Sons of a Bitch

A Novella by
Anthony D. Carr

PHYLLIS,
ENJOY A BIT
OF MY SOUL AS
YOU READ MY BOOK!

8/06

ACARRA Publishing

ACARRA Publishing
5 East Superior
Chicago, Illinois 60611
For information regarding special discounts
or bulk purchases, please call 312.217.5254
E-mail the author at tonycarr50@hotmail.com

*This book is dedicated to the scores
of women that have endured
a son of a bitch, gotten through to
him, and made him her own.*

CHAPTER 1
PROLOGUE

There is no better smell to wake up to in the morning than the smell of drying sex steaming in the early morning air. The lingering smell of sex was affecting Len Edward's ability to sleep. Still trying to fight the smell's affect, Len used all of his will to force himself not to reach between his legs. There throbbing between his legs was a pain that needed to be eased. However, there was no mental way to ease the throbbing while the smell lingered in the air. It was too late; the scent was all in his head.

Trying to find some comfort, Len made the mistake of moving his hand around their bodies to pull the bed covers up around his neck. The effect of doing so caused the scent that was loosely embedded on his hands to dislodge and intensify the early morning air.

The odor stirring in his head forced him to remember. Just hours before his hands roamed over and into his bedmate Tracie's firm body. It was there that his hands picked up the scent of sweat intermixed with perfume and sex.

Enjoying the pleasure that his memory and the scent in the air gave him, Len placed his fingers under his nose and inhaled deeply. His will power now gone, his hands began to do their best between his legs. It was not enough. His hands needed help.

———————————

Fast asleep and purring besides Len, unaware of the growing need that was raging in the man that she laid next to, was Tracie Brown. All who had ever met her noticed the vast contrast between the near flawlessness of her almost jet black skin tone, that covered her athletic body, and her pot-holed covered face. Tracie's face wore, in full effect, the scars of a serious teenage acne problem.

Behind her back, many of her so called friends referred to her as being butt-ugly. A term usually reserved for an unattractive man. Had Tracie's face belonged to a man, it and her five foot ten inch frame would have been considered handsome and desirable to many women. On the other hand, as a woman, her looks handicapped her with romance with men.

It hurt her heart when she thought that most of her female contemporaries already had what she wanted. They were already married with children.

Saddled with her handicap, Tracie over the years endured man after man who wanted nothing more than to try a ride on what was the best body they had ever encountered.

Over time Tracie adapted herself to accommodate her handicap. Clearly, she was not like many other women who spent an excessive amount of time and effort on their hair and face while leaving their bodies to ruin. She kept up with a daily early morning workout routine that would challenge most men that were into their fitness.

Complimenting her body, Tracie was blessed with strong jet-black hair that flowed freely down her head and ended at her upper back. Her hair told of her family's ancestral mixture with the people of Oklahoma's Indian territory. Her hair was truly her pride and joy. However, to her dismay, her body, her hair, and even watching over seventeen years of Oprah were not enough for her to fully overcome her handicap.

In spite of everything that she had done to overcome, still her handicap did not readily lend itself to finding a husband or for that matter even a steady boyfriend – at least not one of the caliber that she had dreamed. Not ready to settle on just any man, most of her experience with men consisted of one-night stands or late night booty calls. It was the results of those relationships that jaded and hardened Tracie against men.

At this point in Tracie's life she accepted men for tools of pleasure; they meant nothing more to her. Just as she was becoming comfortable with her status with men, out of the blue, at a friend's funeral, up pops Len breaking her routine. He put the hard press on her. With his eagerness, for the first time in her life she was in control of her romantic life. She said when, she said how and she said where. She knew that she shouldn't have gotten involved with Len with him being her dead lover's friend and all but she needed to. "A girl has needs doesn't she" is what she said to herself to get over her guilt. Besides, he was so gorgeous.

Len was six foot one and lanky. His skin was lemony in color and revealed a contrasting weathering that told of his age. His hazel eyes perfectly complemented his sandy dark brown closely cropped wavy hair. When his full baritone voice flowed from his full lips into her waiting ears she didn't have a chance. Just like that, without an effort, she completely forgot about a dead love and leaped into a relationship that she hoped would have a future.

Len didn't want or need any foreplay. He was ready. Kissing and hugging were out of the question. He didn't need it again or want it again from his bed mate. Somehow, a softer side of him allowed him to take the time to admire Tracie's flesh. Her body resembled a perfect work of art. Needing what he needed, Len licked his fingers and reached to deposit his saliva between Tracie's legs. Skillfully – knowing how to get what he needed – he repeated the licking of his fingers and a light stroking of her cat until it was wet. The taste of her and him deposited into his mouth from his fingers had him going.

Tracie woke from a deep sleep feeling fingers between her legs. Even still half asleep, she knew better than to turn down some good dick. Needing Len to be the man that she knew that he could be, she laid perfectly still with her breathing uninterrupted pretending to still be sleep.

Tracie savored the moment. It wasn't often, before she started dating Len, that she went to bed with someone and woke up to him the next morning.

Knowing her role like the back of her hand, Tracie lay quietly and smiled to herself in anticipation while letting Len get her ready. As Len moved her body to a good position, she let her weight hang dead allowing him to do his work. She knew that he was going to be good and she wasn't going to turn down good for anything. She needed good and knowing that she was going to get what she needed was priceless to her.

Len wanted it bad. After the last lick and rub, he could feel it trembling between his fingertips. It was ready. Len took the time to touch what he wanted again. This type of approach was not new to him. Just to be sure he licked his fingers one last time and tasted them. The sweet tart flavor from his fingers readily excited his taste buds and drove the thought of rubbing it anymore right out of his mind.

In an instant, his manhood was fully inserted and he was rocking rhythmically while laying side by side with Tracie. There, working it from the side, he could feel her cat grabbing hold of him as he reached the apex of each of his gyrations. Before he wanted to, he was wildly vibrating with his explosion emanate. Len didn't hold back and relented to nature.

Len got his and most times this would have been enough. However, this time, just as he was letting go, Tracie's body began to respond and Len's animal nature took over. Her sway began to move perfectly with his and provided just the right amount of friction to restart and begin anew. Now Len began to move like a cat with prey in mouth. He flipped Tracie over and stayed inserted. Still not quite hard enough; he did what it took to stay inside of her.

Seconds later, his efforts started paying off. With his eyes wide shut, Len took his mind somewhere else. His mind became fixed on a lost past love. Now filling her nicely, skillfully he starting doing what he did best. It was a slow grind. He was adept at doing the fast hard bruising thing and was good at it; but it didn't show off his best side. Len was skilled at hitting just the right spots. He was doing it slowly with a grace that most times is reserved for a lover that one truly loves.

The pace of the grind began to build until it became a gallop. A soft moan came from deep within Tracie forcing Len to further heat things up. In hard and deep, a fast roll, all the way out, let it rub her clit, and back in hard again. The fact that Tracie's chipped nails were now wedged deep in his back told Len that he was "in right."

The nails clawing into his back coupled with his distant thoughts did something to him. He got his second one and still stood tall ready to ride. Unlike him, the gallop became hard, harder, hardest. He was beginning to hurt her.

Tracie wanted so to please. She tried to anticipate his motions and ride out his fury. She was relieved when she felt him release. Her relief was short lived because he didn't stop driving into her.

"Get it baby," she uttered between poundings.

The continued banging of his body into hers was the only reply that she heard. A few seconds dragged by and she could take no more.

"Len you're hurting me," Tracie screamed in a sound that could wake the dead.

Not hearing a thing outside of his own thoughts, Len continued to beat-up what should have been taken with care.

The phone rang until it was tired of ringing. Len continued to lie in the bed in a half sleep half awake state. Answering the phone was the last thing on his mind. He looked over at Tracie lying nestled next him to confirm that the dull hum of the phone's ringer was not disturbing her. She lay like an angel sleeping next to him. Her current angelic state a sharp contrast to the torrid sex that they had been engaged in not twenty minutes earlier.

The phone quit ringing and Tracie still lay with one leg still draped over Len's torso with her face snuggled deep in his armpit. Now, fully awake, Len became fully aware that he didn't want this moment to end. All the sex that they had engaged in earlier could not compare to the quiet ecstasy that was upon him now.

For Len, unlike most men, there was something better than pure sex. He craved the physical contact of a woman's embrace. More important for him was a woman feeling comfortable enough to put her guard down fully and fall asleep in his arms under his care and comfort.

Experience showed him that each woman was a little different. Some twisted and turned in their sleep; some fell fast asleep and of course the worst ones didn't sleep at all. The ones that didn't sleep were only in the bed long enough to work on a repeat performance.

———————

Tracie woke not wanting to move a bone in her body. After the physical beating that she took from Len, she knew that she was going to be sore. However, she didn't mind since she had deep inside of her what she needed. It was the right time, the right place, and the right man. The seed was planted. The rest was up to luck, time, and nature.

NINE MONTHS LATER

CHAPTER 2

US-MA

"Shit had I known that letting go could feel this good I would have let go a long time ago," Maxine Edwards thought to herself.

For sixty-two years she dealt with all that life could throw at her. Somehow, through it all, she prevailed. However, prevailing had its price. Over the years Maxine became jaded and hardened. The changes that came over her and her feelings didn't occur all at one time. They occurred little by little, heartache after heartache, disappointment after disappointment, until what she became resembled nothing like the dark berry colored wide eyed country girl that came up from the south over forty-two years ago.

Maxine continued to enjoy her newfound feeling – or was it new. The feeling was a relief. It was not natural for a woman to have bore two children and feel the way that she felt about life. Thinking back – feeling back – it came to her. She had felt like this once before. However, she couldn't put her finger on when.

The feeling was certainly with me before I got involved with that good looking red-bone man who filled me up with Len, she strained to remember. Was it before my chocolate man talked me into the back seat of his old rusty black on black duce and a quarter? I remember that it was in that duce that Maurice was consummated, she continued with her thoughts. Thoughts that revealed a fondness that she had forgotten existed for Maurice's father.

I remember my family forbidding me from seeing him. When they found out that I was pregnant, they all said it was a sin and wrong. While they were ripping me from him, my sixteen-year old mind was unable to fathom how feeling the way that I did about the baby inside of me and my second cousin could be wrong. At that time my heart was still able to give and accept love.

The feeling had to be before that. I remember straining to forget the shame of it all. It was just as I started showing with Maurice that my mother, at my father's insistence, packed me up and sent me up Route 66 north to Chicago. I couldn't allow Maurice to know his father was also his third cousin.

Over the years I made up lie after lie about his father to keep him from knowing and being badmouthed like I was. I remember all the nights that I laid awake hoping that he would come and save us from the horrors of the big city.

He never came and we never heard from him again. No, I had to have had this feeling before that. It just isn't coming to me. No matter how hard I try I can't put my hands on just when it was that I felt like this.

I can't keep on trying to recall because I'm sure that I have something to do and somewhere to go. But I don't want to go. I don't know if I leave whether or not the way that I am feeling will also leave. I've only had this feeling back with me for a little while but I don't have any idea how I ever functioned without it. But I need to go because I just know that I have something that I'm suppose to be doing. Let me remember; oh please let me remember.

———————————

She didn't want to go because she didn't know if she left whether or not her newly recovered feeling would also leave. The feeling had only been with her for a little while but she was hard pressed to recall how she ever managed without it. Deep inside she also knew that there was some unfinished business so she lingered.

Now with her case hardened exterior gone, she was able to see just how compromised her true womanly charms had been. With her heart as light as a newborns, Maxine reflected over her past. Her thoughts and memories surprised her. She realized just how long she had gone without feeling. Her heart was saddened by the realization that she had selfishly withheld her real essence from everyone in an effort to protect herself from emotional pain.

Maxine needed to do something about what she had done to her sons. Was it too late she thought to herself? She needed to let them know that she had given them all that she could muster at the time but there was so much more inside of her. Sure, she was hard on them. Her memory allowed her to remember that she was especially malicious to Len. She didn't mean to be. He looked too damn much like his jackass of a father.

———————————

My little dark baby Maurice was going to have it hard as he grew up. I tried to love him just a little harder because I knew that he was going to have to depend on that love to be able to cope with the hate and disappointment that this world places on dark skinned black boys. Light skinned people always have it too easy!

I know that most people don't believe that dark skinned people have it hard. But, I know they do. Growing up in the south, I saw it with my own two eyes and felt its pain in my heart. Those light skinned people always got the easy jobs clerking in the stores or something like that while we had to work in the fields or up in somebody's kitchen.

Lord knows that I did my best with those boys. I mean the best that would come out of me, I reflected almost at the verge of dry tears. But they were so different. I can't count the times that somebody would ask me if they were really brothers. I can see why they would ask but at least have the decency not to ask me if they have the same father.

Damn, even Stevie Wonder could see that they didn't. Maurice, my oldest boy, is a rich deep coal black color while Len is as high yellow as high yellow can be. Maurice has always been so fragile. He always needed my help and my reassurance. No matter what was going on, my heart was always able to reach out to him. Don't get me wrong; I love both of my sons. It's just that I have a different feeling about the two of them.

I just bonded right away with little Maurice. After sixteen hours of labor, fresh from my insides, when I saw him, I knew just what he needed. As soon as I saw my baby, I knew that he was going to need all the love that I could muster. I think that's why he tried to stay inside of me for so long. I wanted to give all of my love to him. The type of love that I didn't get when I was growing up.

Even right now, I feel that he needs me to reach out to him and hug and baby him up. I know that it's too late for that now. He's a grown boy now and I've learned my lesson. Love can hurt if not applied right.

After I had Maurice I needed to work. Like a fool I thought it would be all right to leave him with my great aunt and uncle while I did live-in maid work for a family in Hinsdale. It was hard being away from him but I had to do it. It took me half of the one day that I had off from work to get from Hinsdale to 47th Street in the city on public transportation to see my son. I did it for about two months before my loving great aunt and uncle turned on me.

I couldn't believe that they thought that I would agree to give them my baby to raise. I would have rather died first. You know that I gathered up my few things and got out of there. Haven't seen them since. It's bad when you can't trust family. Them trying to take Maurice from me took a lot out of me. What they took I haven't ever been able to get back.

It was hard staying in flats that were no better than flop houses – sometimes with people that I barely knew – washing the dirty drawers, of people who would just as well spit on you, just to have food money for that day. I did it because Maurice was my heart. During that time, he was growing so fast and looking like his father more and more every day. Life was hard then. I didn't know it then but I think we were happy; my baby and me.

Nothing like Maurice, Len slipped right out of me with no trouble at all; I can't even remember any pain at all with him. I could tell from the way that he hurried out of me that he was ready for the world. I was right; as soon as the nurse brought him over to me, I looked down at him and he was as bright as a glowing light bulb. His hazel eyes were wide open. Wouldn't you know that it didn't take long for the talking to start.

"I ain't ever seen a woman as black as her have a baby so white," I heard one of the nurses say loud enough for a deaf man to hear.

She was a black woman talking to another black nurse. They thought that I couldn't hear them but I could. I still acted like I couldn't and just listened some more.

"His daddy must be white," the second nurse whispered matter-of-factly to the other.

"Um uh – must be," the first nurse quietly agreed while nodding her head.

I should have known better than to come to backward ass Cook County Hospital to have a baby. I tried not to let their words hurt me but they did. You knew from the way that they were talking that those two weren't from down south. If they had been then they would have known that you couldn't just judge the skin tone of a baby when it's first born. If you just had to judge, the best place to look at is the edge of the baby's ears – the baby is sure to darken up to at least that color. You'd think that they would know better being delivery room nurses and all.

After what the nurses said, I couldn't help myself. As soon as they handed Len to me, I just had to look at his ears. I remember hoping that maybe he would get a little darker than what his ears showed. I didn't get my wish. It didn't matter, I knew that Len wouldn't need me like my baby Maurice did. Light skinned blacks always have it too easy while we carry the load for the race.

Len and I stayed in the hospital for two days. When it was time to leave, we couldn't even get out of the hospital for all of them nurses cooing over Len and whatnot like he was the second coming. It just sent a chill down my spine watching them. It reminded me of how all of them women used to throw themselves at his father like I wasn't even standing there.

Yes, Len's father is black. I mean if you call having a white father and a light, almost white, black woman for a mother, then black he is. I can almost see Len's father right now with his slicked-back, golden hair, gray eyes, and full revealing lips. He was only the second man that I even looked at twice in my life.

Everybody thought that I liked him because he was light skinned and all. It wasn't that at all. I just loved the way that his behind filled up his pants. It didn't hurt that he was tall – oh about six foot two; but after seeing that ass in those pants coupled with his full lips there was no doubt that this was a black man for my heart.

When he first came up to me and started talking, right there on 43rd street, I couldn't believe it. I felt so lucky; this fine piece of man wanted to take me out on the town. I had to stop and make sure that he was really talking to me. He told me that he was going places and that he would take me with him if I wanted to go.

We had fun for a while – I mean a lot of fun. I remember in his convertible Cadillac coup I performed flawlessly, all the time thinking about the good part that would come. In a forest preserve, late at night, hidden from view, car door flung open, lying across the car's front bench seat, I opened up and let him in. Flat on my back, knees way wide, I let him love me. He was good too.

I didn't know it then but time has taught me that some men just know how to handle a woman. Experience can only teach a man so much about how to work that thang; the rest comes from a man's passion. Either he has it or he doesn't. Woo, let me tell you that that man had it when it came to moving his ass.

Going places? You know that I wanted to go. So, when he lightly pressed the back of my head forcing me for the first time to look at a man's thang, I didn't resist. Instinct made me reach out and touch the tip of it. Right before my eyes it seemed like it got twice as big.

He guided one of my hands to his balls and moved my fingers to slightly squeeze them while he worked my other hand over the length of it. It was smooth to the touch and once I started moving my hands up and down it and saw the effect that it had on him, I didn't want to stop touching it. Seconds later, he removed my hand from its job and motioned for me to come closer to him.

Before I knew it, his hand was on the nape of my neck tugging lightly. I wanted to please, so I allowed him to push my head downward. I opened my mouth and tasted him. I expected it to have a taste to it. It surprised me that it was plain. I did like it though. I especially liked the warmth of him filling my mouth, the smoothness of the skin, and how it pulsated and grew right inside of my mouth. It felt so good that if I knew what I was doing, as much as I was enjoying the feeling, I know that I would have turned him out.

Needless to say, over the next few minutes I got a little better at my new job. Without any warning, all of a sudden he pushed my head back from him. It squirted everywhere. All I can remember thinking and unwillingly saying was, "Oh you made a mess," in a mannish matronly tone. I took my time and cleaned him up with my tongue and before I knew it was filling my mouth again. I made sure that there were no more messes – you know they say that an ounce of prevention is worth a pound of cure.

After he was through, I was doing my best to reassemble my clothes while he was outside the car I think going to the bathroom or something. No sooner did he get back to the car then he began pulling at me again. I didn't care that he was a little rough. I liked that he couldn't get enough of me. I thought that we were perfect together and I was going to give him what he needed. As his force came down on me, his size pushed the air out of me causing an embarrassing sound like a loud fart.

As he got going, I lost control of my mouth. It took on the established rhythm of our love making and began saying, "Ain't my pussy good? Ain't my pussy good?" I don't know where the words came from but I keep repeating them in time. I didn't need an answer. The way that he rolled inside of me and the hump in his back answered my question in the affirmative. Each of his thrusts coarsely said, "You've got some good pussy. You've got some really good pussy." I loved the way his thrusts into me said it over and over again.

He was hard at work, the sweat ran down his face and dripped on me. The first drop that I noticed actually ran down his face, came off his chin, and landed in my mouth. It didn't stop my mouth though – it was on automatic; "Ain't my pussy good? Ain't my pussy good?" Getting close to where every woman wants to get, the sound coming from my mouth changed from words to moans and squeals.

As his sweat continued to drip off of his face, I let one hand slip off of his humping ass and grabbed the hem of my dress, that was now resting around my shoulders, to wipe the sweat from his face, neck, and hairy chest. Letting go of the dress, I took the opportunity to let my finger tips address his nipples that were revealed after I unbuttoned his shirt. Why did I do that? Instantly – for just like a very hard rain, a recklessly fast and hard fuck can't last too long – he came.

He pulled out of me and a few moments later I reached in and removed what was left of a prophylactic from inside of me.

It wasn't even a week after he took me in the car that I saw them together. She was darker than me with a long neck like a pelican sitting there in his car where we had did the unmentionable; sitting where I was supposed to be.

Later that night I found them at the Blue Note Blues Bar and Fried Chicken Hut on South Chicago Ave. I just needed to see what was going on. Maybe they were just friends I thought to myself.

Once inside of the bar, I sat on the other side of the room and watched as the heifer reached out and rubbed the back of his neck. I was still there as they were dancing so close that it seemed that they were one person; not two. I watched as she laid her head on his chest in mock exhaustion and then lifted her chin in anticipation of a kiss from him. She was getting my kiss. I started to lose it. Somehow, I pulled it together but I don't know how I held it together.

I didn't need to see anymore. I calmly left the club unnoticed by either one of them with it all building up inside of me. I didn't explode – I got even. The next night I found his car and poured three bottles of Kayro syrup into its gas tank. My friend Zephyr told me that one bottle would do the trick to seize his car's engine but just to be on the safe side I used three. I don't think the damn fool ever knew that it was me who did it – at least he didn't say anything about it.

I even let him take me out again one last time a month or two after I had did that to his car. I told him that I wanted to go to Mrs. Mary's restaurant for dinner. Mrs. Mary, God rest her soul, had the best fried chicken in all of Bronzeville. For effect, I made sure that I looked as good as Mrs. Mary's chicken always tasted. I needed him to see the best of me.

When we got to Mrs. Mary's, we got ourselves a table and he ordered a setup of scotch. I settled into one of the booths that was crowded into what at onetime was someone's front room in the gray-stone turned restaurant.

Mrs. Mary, like many black entrepreneurs of her day, started selling her food right out of the pots when she began keeping boarders in her home to make ends meet over thirty years before then. There was no shortage of people in Chicago that wanted a good home cooked meal at a reasonable price.

Almost overnight Mrs. Mary was feeding well over thirty people a night. Over the years, the kitchen was expanded and booths and tables were added to the first floor front room of the gray-stone. Anybody could eat in the kitchen but you had to be neatly dressed to sit in the front room.

There was no menu at Mrs. Mary's place. You just knew by the day of the week what she was going to be cooking. The only thing that was cooked every day was fried chicken. It had to be a Thursday that we went to Mrs. Mary's because I ordered a half chicken fried, another half chicken smothered, and some liver and onions to boot. You see, Mrs. Mary only serves liver and onions on Thursdays. When the food came it was enough food for at least four or five people.

Just to make sure that he didn't mind how much food I was ordering, I let his hand rest on my thigh as I ordered. While I ate, he just sat there next to me trying to inch his hand up a little higher under my skirt on my thigh. I already knew what he wasn't going to be doing that night so I just let him inch his hand up a little higher on my leg. I allowed him to go just high enough to get him going but I didn't let him touch the good stuff though.

We ate and drank until I couldn't eat or drink anymore. After we ate, I told him that I wanted to go dancing. I wanted everybody to see us and I hoped that long necked pelican woman would be there so that she could see what a real woman looked like.

Would you believe that classless bastard took me to the same joint that he had taken the pelican. I put that out of my mind; I didn't care. I was on the dance floor. I wanted everyone to see. I wanted them to see the before and the after.

Come to think of it – you know before I began to feel like I did before – I used to love to dance. I guess it's all water under the bridge now. Anyway, I was having a good ole time dancing and strutting my stuff around.

After we sat down from dancing, just in case he had any doubt, I unbuttoned two more of the buttons on my blouse so that he could see a little more of me. It wasn't too long after we finished on the floor that he leaned over close to me and whispered into my ear that he wanted to get a room out in back of the spot. I didn't know then but I know now that those rooms out back were mainly used by men that were too cheap to get a better place or by women that needed money so bad that they didn't mind the rat infested hole in the wall accommodations.

No! No not me! I told that bastard that I didn't need no room because I had an apartment that I could do whatever I wanted to do in. I said it while rubbing my chest for effect. I let the tips of my fingers slip into the top of my blouse and saw his eyes open wide in longing. He was ready for me to put him down hard and baby I was up to the task.

The engine in his car was still locked up from the Kayro syrup so we had to take a cab from the Blue Note. About half way to my house he began to try to kiss me and tried to rub on my tatas. I wasn't having any of it; I pushed him off of me under the cab driver's watchful eye. None too soon, the cab pulled up to my apartment building and he started to pay the driver.

"You don't have to get out," I told him already pushing my own door open to make my exit. "You can take this cab to your whore's house!"

"What are you talking about Max?"

He said it like he was really concerned. You know by then I didn't care to hear anything that came out of his mouth. Now fully out of the cab I was free to give him a piece of my mind. He beat me to it while he was coming towards me.

"You bitch you owe me and I'm coming up to your apartment."

"I don't owe you a damn thing! I've already given you what I owe you. Your car; I did…"

My words were cut off with the recoil of my head on my neck. I remember the slap but that's about all I remember.

I woke-up the next morning admitted into Cook County Hospital. The doctor told me that I was lucky. He said that if I would have hit my head on the ground two inches lower on the back of my head that neither me nor my baby would have been here today.

I remember asking in surprise, "What does this have to do with my baby he's with the sitter isn't he?"

"Oh! You don't know!" The young doctor stated in a surprised tone.

"Know what!" I demanded focused on the well being of Maurice.

In the next few seconds I was hit on the head again. This one didn't knock me out but it hurt just the same. I must have cried a river. I was pregnant. I didn't want to be but I was.

I left the hospital later that day. I never saw his father again and he never knew about Len. Why should he? We didn't need any weak minded, can't keep his thing in his pants, good for nothing man anyway. I had Len seven months later. I tried to get over the hurt of his father and put it out of my mind. But every time Len cried or looked me in my eyes, the hurt that his father put in me just came to the surface. I think most people can deal with that type of pain; I did the best that I could.

After Len was born, my boys and I settled into one of the high-rise Cabrini Green buildings on Chicago's near north side. Trying to live, let alone raise two boys, in a high-rise project was hard. I didn't have anything to go by; I was raised in the country. Around these damn projects there's only concrete and packed dirt mounds where grass and trees should be.

Just trying to find a good switch – like the ones that my momma would have us get when I was a kid from the maple tree out at the edge of the field behind our Columbus, Mississippi house – was next to impossible; they were hard to come by. I can still remember like it was yesterday some of my slow walks out to that tree.

Momma would say, when she got good'n mad at me or one of my brothers, "Get out there and get me a switch! I'ma beat the black right off of your ass."

Right then the walk out to that maple tree would start. After finally getting to the tree, I would take my time picking out a limb from the low hanging branches of the tree.

The limb had to be not too strong or too stiff or too flexible or too long or too short. After going through about twenty or so branches, I would break off one of the limbs and hold it in my hands wondering if I could talk my way out of the pending whipping that was going to happen when I got back to the house.

Slowly, against my will, one by one I would pick each leaf off of the branch. By the time that the switch was ready, I wasn't. Nobody is ever ready for a whipping. So I would just have a seat right there under that tree and contemplate a way out. Maybe she would forget all about the switch and I would be saved. It never worked; momma always came out to that tree looking for me. Yep! I can still remember like it was yesterday some of those whippings out there by that tree.

Now, with no good trees around the projects, it is almost impossible to find a good switch when you need one to get a child back in line. Maurice wasn't that bad but that Len started talking back and being mannish almost as soon as he could talk. I just wasn't ready for how Len showed out all of the time. When Maurice was his age he was so quiet and respectful. Even when he did get into something it was never really that bad. But that Len – umh, umh, umh – just could not do like he was told.

Almost from the start, my hand just wasn't enough with Len. By the time that he was nine I had switched from a thick leather belt to an extension cord. The extension cord helped some; especially when he was around me. When he was at school that was another story all together.

I got note after note sent home to me from the school. There were never any notes about his school work – Len was always an excellent student – it was always Len's behavior that the notes complained about. One day, after getting a phone call from the principal's office about Len, I had enough. I just marched right down to that school with my extension cord in my hand and took care of Len right then and there. That did the trick; after that I didn't get any more notes from the school.

When it came to school, that Maurice didn't give me a lick of trouble. He brought me home good grades year after year and never a note of complaint. You can't blame me for rewarding that can you? I mean when a child does what he is supposed to do he's suppose to get rewarded; and when a child acts up with me he doesn't get shit.

Boy, let me tell you that-that boy Len did some acting up. I remember when he was about fourteen. I came home from the little part time job that I had found at the Jewel Food Store down on Clark and Division streets and found that boy humping his little ass up and down on top of some grown ass girl.

He was doing it right there in the middle of the front room floor. I looked down at them and saw that it was the grown ass girl that lived in the apartment down the hall. It had been going around the building the past few weeks how she was supporting her entire family including her momma's drug habit on her back.

I was so shocked to see him down there humping and grunting that I was frozen in place for what seemed like a year. His pants and draws pulled down and gathered around his skinny legs and ankles. Would you believe that that boy didn't even notice me standing right over them.

That woman-child noticed me first. "Cuse Me!" Spat out of her mouth liked I had just walked into her apartment.

I snapped and before I knew it in one hand I had a broomstick and in the other I had the clothes iron ready to do battle.

I got them both cornered in the kitchen and I beat both of them like there was no tomorrow with that stick and iron. She ran out of my apartment into the hallway with nothing on except one sock. I told Len to get in his room and that I didn't ever want to see his face again. During all this time Maurice was safely tucked inside my room watching TV just like a good kid should be when his momma is out hard at work trying to keep a roof over his head and food on his plate.

After what I had been through I needed a drink. I had Maurice pour my usual Old Grand Dad 100 proof and grape fruit juice in a tall tumbler and bring it to me. A few sips later I settled down from all of the excitement and Maurice came in and talked to me. Can you believe that that boy wanted me to whip him and put him on punishment for what his brother had done with that girl. Said that he was as guilty as Len was. Ain't that something how that boy would try to take up for his brother.

I tell you; when you have a good child you can't help but love him a little harder. I reached right out and hugged him to me right then and there. Maurice and me popped popcorn, watched TV, and drank all night. I had Old Grand Dad 100 proof and grapefruit juice while he had Kool-aid. Len was in the back in the room on punishment.

———————————

I don't have to tell you that I couldn't wait for those boys to grow up and get out of my house. Hell, I wanted my life back. You can't have no life with two boys watching your every move. I had to give up my life for them. I never really considered getting married because of them.

Don't get me wrong, I had me some friends over the years and we went out and everything. I made sure that when they would take me home, that the boys were sleep before I would let them touch me. Most of the time I didn't even want a man to touch me. But you know that after a man treats you to a movie and a bag of popcorn he's gonna want something. A few times, I had to do it out of necessity.

The short squat white man that came to cut off the gas – I just closed my eyes and just like that I was back down south in the back seat of that old Buick all over again. I had to concentrate on what I was doing when it came to the butcher's monthly visit. He always brought two big brown paper bags of groceries with him. One was filled with meat and the other was filled with dry goods. I had to be good and take care of him right because I needed him to keep coming back with those bags. Men are so easy when you don't fall for them. So with the butcher I kept my mind on what I was doing.

The butcher thought that he was getting all the pussy; dumb ass man. As soon as the butcher got to my place I would fix him a strong drink. Before he could take a good sip of the drink I would have him on the couch working his dick with my hands. A few more sips of the drink and then I'd start to let him work on trying to get my clothes off.

Before he got to the house I would make sure that I had on something with a lot of buttons. All the while that he was struggling with those buttons trying to get my clothes off, if he wasn't grinding his jimmy on me, I was working that thang with my hand. I'll be damned if I was going to let him fuck the shit out of me. I was even lucky a few times and got away with not giving him any pussy at all because he came right in my hand. With the drink and his release working on him he was done. He might sleep for an hour after that.

If he didn't come in my hand, by the time he made it through all of the clothes that I had on and got his fat ass on top of me, he was only good for five or six – never more than ten – pumps and he was finished. Like I said, he thought that he was getting all the pussy. I had what I needed. Nope, his little dick wasn't even beginning to make a cuchie feel anything. When he woke up an hour or so later, I would be pretending to be sleep. I didn't want him to get any ideas that he was getting any more of my stuff.

Seeing that I was sleep, he would put on his clothes being as quiet as a church mouse, leave a twenty on the end table turned night stand, and be gone. I would get up after he left and take the hottest shower that I could stand and then go back to bed.

It went on like that with the butcher like clock work every twenty-eight days or so. I know that he was keeping up with my periods so that he wouldn't get caught up with some half breed kid looking like him. The butcher didn't know it but he didn't have anything to worry about. I was careful because I didn't need any more mouths to feed. After Len, I only slipped up twice. I went to the clinic and had it taken care of both times. After that, I just had my tubes tied. Like I said, I didn't need any more mouths to feed. Good thing that the butcher didn't know about those tubes, he might have wanted some sex every night.

You know that my damn check and those food stamps never went far enough. After I started smoking I had to have a pack a day. Every now and then, I needed to escape so I had to be able to afford a shot or two of Old Grand Dad 100 proof so that I didn't go crazy. There never was enough money to go around.

I guess Len could feel that he was the odd man out because when he turned eleven he got himself a paper route. Maurice tried his hand at one too but it didn't stick with him. I thought it was for the best since when he got grown he would have to work hard for the rest of his life anyway. Before too long, Len was doing his paper route, Maurice's old route, and a third one too. That was just way too much money for an eleven year old so I held his money for him and put him on a five dollar a week allowance. He didn't need any more money than that.

At first I told him that I was just holding the money for him. Before I knew it, I was dipping into the money that I was holding for him. It was just a little for this and a little for that. Shit that money came in handy. Food stamps and my little check only went so far. Who would have ever thought that an eleven year old was keeping up with how much money he had made. You know that I almost had a fit when about a year later Len came and asked me about getting some of the five hundred forty-two dollars that I was holding for him.

"How much do you think that it cost to put clothes on your back and feed you," I asked a twelve year old. "Ain't nothing free," I said with the resolve of someone who could not make good on the debt that was owed to her own flesh and blood.

He didn't have any reply. The look on his face told all. And you know what? For the first time I understood that my boy Len had a backbone and a brain because he never gave me any more money to hold for him.

Without me looking forward those boys were grown. I haven't seen Len in almost two years. I hope that he understands and doesn't hate me. I just couldn't see before now. My baby Maurice; I have tried so hard but he just seems to be drifting. Now that I know better; I need to do something. I feel like I can do it too. This feeling is so good nothing can stop me.

CHAPTER 3

MAURICE

Maurice Edwards over the last three days and nights had been to hell and back and was still clueless where he was going next. Feeling his monkey square on his back.

Maurice laid as still as a dead man while wrapped tightly in a thread bare blanket atop a foam mattress. Both the blanket and the mattress were issued to him just after his arrival two nights ago to this man-made hell known as Cook County Jail.

The inch and a half thick, two foot wide foam mat covered just about all of Maurice's allotted personal space on the cold hard concrete dayroom floor. It was hard resting on the dayroom floor because the mat he laid on provided almost no comfort at all from the cool hardness of the floor.

Many of the other inmates in the cell block, who did not have cots, enjoyed more personal space and most had two sometimes three of the mats stacked one on top of another for extra comfort. They enjoyed this extra because they held a status among the other inmates that afforded them a certain rank. Their rank was hard won from being in hell with some of the hardest heads in all of Cook County.

As a newbie in the jail, Maurice was at the bottom of the food chain when it came to rank. It didn't take long for another inmate to make sure that Maurice knew his place.

"Hey man you in my spot," a gorilla looking man that had to be at least six foot five inches tall and three hundred fifty pounds impressed to Maurice before he could get his mat rolled out good.

Maurice, a slim build man, stood all of five foot nine inches tall if you stretched it with his shoes on, apprised his situation. In an instant, even though he was still feeling the effects of a fifth of Demitri gin and three crack rocks that he had consumed that day, he understood that he didn't want to tangle with this giant of a man.

"I'm sorry man. This is where the guard told me to go," Maurice demurely stated trying not to inflame the situation.

"Naw man. You new guys s'pose to sleep standing up," the big man stated with a smirk on his face in a tone as if he owned everything in the entire cellblock.

Maurice had never been in jail before but he knew the streets well. His street sense told him that if he didn't stand up to this guy he would be the big guy's bitch and be answering to him as long as he was in this place.

"Man that's fucked up," Maurice replied looking dead in his prey's eyes. "I guess I'll have to stay right here then," he stated never removing his eyes from their task of staring at the man's body language. The twitch on the big man's face told Maurice what he had to do.

The first punch landed right between the big man's eyes; right above his nose. Maurice's foot in the man's groin was enough to put the big man down. Maurice was quick and efficient in his movement against the big man.

The big man never had a chance to respond – surprise coupled with very little to no talking and puffing was Maurice's secret weapon when it came to a street fight.

There was never a reason to let your victim know that you were coming. Unknown to Maurice, until it was too late, his victim came with back-up. The giant had fallen but his two smaller friends were now working Maurice over. One of them had a hold of him while the other landed punch after body punch knocking the fire out of Maurice's body.

"Who in the hell do you think you are coming in here trying to take over," the smaller of the two men asked between punches to Maurice's kidneys. "We run this shit."

Maurice couldn't respond or answer. He was finished after a sharp right ripped through his insides. Moments later the altercation was over. Maurice had won a place to sleep but it had come with a price.

Now, Maurice continued to lay shielded from terror by being wrapped in the limited safety of his county issued lint riddled blanket cocoon. Not wanting to engage his environment any more than he was forced to, he laid perfectly still holding his eyes closed.

Lying there life began to drain from him. It became evident that there were some environmental issues in his current situation that could not be ignored. For some reason, even though he was using all of his will power to force his senses to leave him alone, so that he could feel nothing, his sense of smell was over powering and betraying him. It was working overtime with a heightened state of sensitivity.

From the lingering thick air, Maurice could discern a pungent odor that told that someone's feet, between their toes, were rotting away from an extreme case of foot fungus. Maurice had never smelled a stench so strong. The smell was nauseating by itself. However, the air also carried the smell of someone who could not have washed their ass in a month of Sundays.

Needing to escape his environment with a quickness, Maurice started to think back. Trying to find relief, he struggled to try and remember how it all came to this. Thinking back with all of his energy, Maurice drifted off into a familiar state of semi-consciousness that had become his friend over the last two nights. However, this time Maurice's un-conscience state was a little different than before. This time Maurice's body also went limp – it just gave up and went dormant.

Unlike his body, Maurice's mind remained active still searching for answers. His mind raced then lingered then raced again. As his mind raced, little by little his thoughts were becoming clear to him. The images in his mind were like a digital re-creation of the past forty-five years of his life. It was all coming back to him; search, pause, play. Over and over again – search, pause, play.

———————————

I can't remember but I was told by my moms and the records say that I was born on January 16. Len and me we call our mother Us-Ma. What I do know is that my mother loved me from the beginning. I was never told who my father is and the records don't say who he is either. Us-Ma always talked about him like he was going to come and get us any day when I was growing up.

When I was little, Us-Ma used to have a picture in a frame that she said was my father. I found out later that the picture in the frame was just a clipping from a magazine. I often asked her about him but each time I asked and Us-Ma told me about him she cried. After a while to stop her from crying and since he was never around, I just stopped asking about him.

I was a good kid really until I had my first drink. My little brother Len – he's three years younger than me – was always into something around the hood. I must have been about sixteen or seventeen when he brought Princess to the crib. Princess lived down the hall from us. A little while before then, her moms had started making her have sex with different men so that they could make ends meet.

Being poor is a mother fucker I guess. By this time nobody had to make Princess do anything anymore; sex was in her blood. Being the oldest, I basically gangstered Princess away from Len. It didn't take much since Len was deathly afraid of Us-Ma. All I had to say was that I was going to tell and he relented her to me. Princess didn't care; there was twenty dollars on the table. I still don't know if she wanted the money or needed it. Right now I guess that doesn't matter; the twenty was all the influence that two kids needed with her. Oh yea, the twenty came from Len's paper route money. That boy somehow always had money – I never did.

Princess was my age – maybe a year younger – and still had a glitter in her eyes that made her pretty. The last time that I saw her that glitter in her eyes was gone; she looked nothing like her former self. Back then, I had always liked her. We useta play together when we were little. You know house and shit like that. Even then, at five or six you knew that she was going to be fine as hell when she grew up.

Rumor had it that one of her moms' boy friends broke her in when she was no more than thirteen. After that her moms said that if she was going to date boys she was going to do it to help around the house like she had been doing for years. I heard that her moms said that it was time for her to retire. So you can see that Princess had some age on her that went beyond her years.

Feeling that I needed to bring something to the party, I eagerly offered up a drink to get things started. I didn't expect anybody to say that they wanted one; I just didn't have anything else to offer other than Us-Ma's liquor. I wasn't putout when Princess said that she wanted one. I had been fixing Us-Ma a drink or two almost every night for the past two or three years.

Instead of the sour grapefruit juice, I mixed grape Kool-Aid in with Old Grand Dad 100 proof and added a lot of ice. Come to think about it now you know the drink tasted a little like a brick of Richards Wild Irish Rose.

Princess and I took turns drinking from the same glass. I took sips from the glass while Princess drank like a sailor. Len didn't drink at all. He went over and turned the radio on while we got our drink on. I remember that Marvin Gaye's *Sexual Healing* was playing.

I sent Len away and started kissing and groping Princess. I started doing the best that my inexperienced mind knew how to do. After a few seconds Princess took over. She raised her tight fitting skirt up just enough so that it wasn't in the way and got on top of me.

I was surprised that she didn't have on any panties. I just laid there dumbfounded not knowing what was expected of me. Even right now I can remember her smell. It was alright. No big deal. It didn't last too long and I was finished.

Long after I was finished, I was still feeling the effects of the Old Grand Dad laced with Kool-Aid. I was hooked and not on sex.

The next day Princess was back. It was Len's turn with her. I remade the Kool-Aid and Old Grand Dad mix the same as the day before. This time I held onto the tumbler a little longer than I did yesterday. My sip of the liquid contents was deeper also. I think that I must have drunk about a quarter of the drink and was on full.

Princess looked better today than she did yesterday to me. I guess what you can't have always looks better to you. She was dressed in a plaid schoolgirl uniform type of getup that was about two sizes too small for her. Her hair was done up in flowing Shirley Temple curls that cupped the perfect skin on her face accenting her high cheekbones. She was flat out sexy.

I left the room so that Len could do his thing. However, I couldn't help myself, from behind the door I had to look at what was going on. They didn't know that I was looking at them but I got an eye full.

Princess was different with Len than she was with me. Len laid back on the front room couch. She came up to him and unbuttoned his shirt and licked his nipples. I saw Len shutter. I think Len was following her lead when he pushed the straps of Princess's school girl outfit off of her shoulders and unbuttoned her blouse and took a hold of one her breasts.

Damn! Princess's face was pretty but her chest was beautiful: it was the first set that I had ever seen. I was rock hard. I remember thinking *why wasn't she like this with me?* She kept kissing Len all over while she took off the rest of her clothes until all she had on was a pair of white bobby socks.

Pants down Len got on top of Princess. He looked like he knew what he was doing. Even if he didn't, he was much better at it than I was. He was down there like he did it to girls every night. It's a bad feeling when your little brother is better than you are at something, especially sex.

It was then that all hell broke loose. I couldn't help Len. I didn't even hear Us-Ma coming; I was too busy looking at what Len was doing. Before I know it, Us-Ma was standing over the two of them with a broomstick and an iron. It got pretty ugly in there. Wasn't nothing I could do. I went into the room and just acted like I had been watching TV all the time. It worked too but I felt so bad that Len got beat and put on punishment. I tried to tell Us-Ma that I was guilty too but she didn't want to believe me.

That night, Us-Ma and me popped popcorn, watched TV, and drank all night. I fixed Us-Ma two or three Old Grand Dad 100 proof and grapefruit juice drinks. Us-Ma didn't know it but I matched her drink for drink that night mixing my grape Kool-Aid with her Old Grand Dad. All the time that we were lounging around having fun, Len was in the back in the room on punishment.

That day taught me two things; that I needed to get better at having sex and the pain of being Len.

Us-Ma spent so much time with me when I was little trying to help me get my school lessons. We would stay-up till all hours of the night doing homework. Len would always have his homework done by the time that Us-Ma got home from wherever she was that day. It didn't matter though; Us-Ma would make him stay up until I got my homework done. Me? From the start I never had to do my homework alone and for some reason I couldn't get focused on it until Us-Ma got home.

I think that Len must have gotten tired of my shit because, by the time that he was eleven, he started reading my school books and doing my homework before I got to it. After awhile, Len got real good at doing my homework. Even not doing my own homework myself, I still got good grades in school. All of my teachers spent extra time with me. I think that they were scared that Us-Ma would come up to the school and pay them a visit. I know that she had to come up to the school on more than one occasion to set a teacher straight about something.

With Us-Ma and me everything was all right. I knew the rules and especially knew not to break the cardinal rule. You didn't lie to Us-Ma. If you got caught lying then you were going to catch all kinds of hell. I didn't ever lie to Us-Ma – I couldn't take the heat. Because of that, still to this day I can't stand for anyone to lie to me. It's time to fight if you do. That's one of the reasons that I got myself locked up now.

We grew up – Len and me. We were never the same again after the Princess situation. We didn't hangout growing up anymore and we don't hangout now. I can't remember the last time that I have even seen him. He turned out real good though. I really miss that boy. I need to find him. I think he needs me right about now. I don't want him to fail like I have.

See, I've been drinking ever since that first drink. The drinking took me away and for a while let me deal with Us- Ma's expectations that I couldn't – I mean didn't want to live up to. Life just moved on. The more Us-Ma pushed the more that I did just enough to get by. Oh, but when I was drunk I was the king of the mountain. The King.

———————————

Four days ago, I started early getting my drink and smoke on. I was hanging with a few of the locals down by the pool hall. I had my own private fifth of gin and wasn't sharing or nursing it at all. From time to time, to ensure that my high stayed on full, I would leave the crowd to go and do a ten dollar rock. By six that night, I was right. I mean I was right and there was nothing that I wanted to do more than get with my girl and grab me a little piece of that ass.

I got to the apartment and can you believe that my woman had a bunch of people there having a get together? That wasn't the worst part of it all. As soon as I opened the door all I can see is her all hugged up slow dancing with some niggrow. Somehow, I don't know how I did it, I stayed calm.

Now, I like a good party as much – I mean more – than the next guy so I just flowed with the scene. I was so zooted up from the drink and crack that I had done that day that the entire party scene seemed surreal but I was OK with it – I think.

After awhile, when I got my girl off to the side, I asked
her, "Who was that nigger that was dancing with you earlier?"

"Oh. Um. It was nobody; you know."

Feeling that what she just told me was a lie but wanting to give her the benefit of the doubt I continued, "Baby nobody don't dance. Who in the hell was that?"

"I told you that it wasn't anybody. What you keep asking me for? You're drunk!" She was getting loud and trying to front me. In my mind there was no reason for her to do either unless something out of the way was going on. I was on the edge now.

"Girl don't fuck with me! If nothing was going on then why did the bastard leave after he saw me. I'ma ask your silly ass one more time. Who in the fuck was that?" I was loud but I couldn't control myself. Like I said, I hate lies and liars; she knows this.

"Go sit your drunk ass down someplace Maurice!"

All I saw was red. I didn't mean to go off and beat her ass with a house full of people there. It could have waited. Damn, I fucked-up – didn't I? It's not the first time. That's why the cops were so damn hard on me. With all the shit that they put in that police report you would think that I was a one-man wreaking crew. Was I? Hell I don't know.

Why couldn't I find a woman that understands me? Someone who's firm when she needs to be firm. Soft when I need her to be soft; a woman who is just all about me. Is that too much to ask? I know what I want. I have felt that way before when I was little and Us-Ma was taking care of me. Why couldn't any of the women that I've dated understand what I needed? Shit; I can't think about that now. I got this feeling that I should be doing something else.

———————

"Hey Ma! What you doing here?" Maurice felt the presence of Us-Ma and acknowledged it.

"Boy, I knew something was wrong. I was right too.

Look at you. It's not supposed to be like this," Maxine started weeping uncontrollably.

"Ma I'm sorry. I'm OK."

"No you're not boy. Don't you know that no mother wants to see a child of hers like this," she replied through her tears. "Come on here boy we've got to find Len."

CHAPTER 4

TRACIE

It was always bad boy types that got me in trouble, Tracie mused concerned about her current dilemma. I don't know why I've always liked them, Tracie continued talking and thinking to herself. They just really get me going. When I saw that number on the caller ID, I should have known better than to answer that phone. I've never said no to Roc before. I don't know what in the world made me think that this time would be any different. That man just has my number. The fact that I had been totally fulfilled earlier that day flew right out of my mind as soon as I heard his voice. When he spoke, I stirred both mentally and physically.

"Hello, baby are you there?" Roc asked into the phone's answering machine.

I remembered the voice that spoke into the answering machine. I couldn't believe that I could feel the voice's effect. I felt its effect even before I had a chance to make up my mind whether or not I was going to pick up the receiver.

I just stood there unsure of how I was going to respond.

My physical and mental being was in conflict with what my brain was telling me not to do.

It wasn't like I needed or even wanted to have sex. All day today, every time I moved any bone in my lower body, I felt the effects of how Len took care of me the night before and again this morning. God knows that I don't know how or why but that voice has a way of getting inside of me. I knew what that voice could do.

Damn, I'm already wet and trembling. Roc's voice continued to do its thing. In a raspy tone it invited, "I was just thinking that if you weren't doing anything that maybe we could do nothing together. Let me know before too long."

My physical and mental overcame my brain and I picked up the phone. "Hey Roc what chu want?"

"You know what I want girl. I want to see you," Roc was working with that voice.

"Roc it's almost that time of the month. I can't be fooling around."

"What's almost girl?"

"Almost is almost! Don't play with me."

"Ok. Lets go to the movies and see that new Denzel flick. You like Denzel don't you?"

"Yea, I do. What time you talk'n about picking me up?"

"I need a fix girl. I'm right around the block. Do you want me to come up now?"

"No-No! I'll be down in about five minutes. Meet me out front."

I took out a straight, a little longer than a mini, brown distressed leather skirt and paired it with a peach colored halter top. A tiger print thong and a pair of brown flat sandals, to show off the pedicure that I pampered myself with, finished off the look. The outfit showed off my fitness and made the best of everything I had. I also knew that Roc liked me to show off my legs when I was with him. I liked that Roc liked to go out with me and show me off so I did my best to wear things that he wanted to see me in.

In less than nine minutes, I was downstairs sitting pretty in the front seat of Roc's STS ready for the night to begin. In the car, Roc wasted no time pulling me close to him; as close as he could with the car's console between us. He smelled good. I could detect the scent of Issey Miyake cologne flowing from him into my nose.

Without a thought of pulling away from the front of my apartment building, Roc had his tongue in my mouth and his hands were trying to spread my crossed legs. I liked a man to be a man so I didn't mind Roc's direct approach but I wasn't going to let him in; I couldn't. Tonight I just wanted to have a little fun. I knew what he wanted to see and what would happen if I let him see it.

He changed up his approach on me and caught me by surprise. During the last three months that we were seeing one another he never paid any attention to my chest. They were small – just barely enough not to feel bad about putting on a B cup but they were very sensitive. He raked his sandpaper like thumb over my left nipple and I melted.

Wet and relaxed, right there in front of my apartment, he eased my legs open, felt how wet I was and saw what he wanted to see.

"What's this girl? You know I don't go for no draws."

Before I could say a word it had happen. He ripped my thong in half at the crotch and had a handful of my middle in his hand. He knew what he was doing; he didn't need to put any fingers inside of me; he just skillfully held me in his hand.

"He was purring inside of my right ear, "You're so damn juicy and soft I can't wait to taste you."

"You better stop boy. I told you what time of the month it was."

"I don't care if it hasn't started then let me bring it down. Let me lick it then hit it."

All the time that he was talking into my right ear he just kept right on gently squeezing and releasing my center and caressing the tip of my left nipple that was now his.

The tremble in my body said it all – the answer was yes. At that time, any thoughts of earlier that day were far removed from my head.

Before I knew it we were back upstairs in my apartment. Now I needed what I wanted so I slipped in one of my hope CDs and was sitting on Roc's thigh just barely moving back and forth giving my thang just a little stimulation.

This was good. I had caught my breath and had a thought that I could get some of what I needed without going too far. Any other time Roc would have already been in my bed licking me all over.

———————————

I'm going to be a woman about this. I'm grown and I should have what I want – shouldn't I? I've gone without enough over the years. I'm going to enjoy this time of plenty for what it's worth.

———————————

Tracie loved how her almost blue black skin blended or contrasted with a lover's skin tone. In less then twelve hours Tracie had experienced the best of both of her desires – one light one dark. They contrasted her and each other; they were both so different but she loved what they both did for her. Anything else just wouldn't do.

Over the entirety of her romantic life, she had never given a brown skin man the time of day. They were shit colored to her and she didn't want any thing to do with them. It was either light bright or blacker than all the midnights combined for her when it came to men. One extreme or the other. There was no middle ground. Roc was the midnight color that she needed right now.

"He sure was something wasn't he?" Tracie whispered to herself almost under her breath feeling not the least bit of shame for her inability to control herself. But that was so unlike me; I am always so very careful.

Tracie thought about her condition and the indiscretion that was the source of her current pain. I guess it was just the flow of the night that caused it. Roc sure was good though, she said as if she was talking to a best girlfriend; she was forced to talk to herself since she had no best girlfriends. She longed for her last girlfriend Kayla. If Kayla was around she would be able to tell her what she should do. With no one else to talk to, Tracie turned to her mother.

I don't know why I told my momma what was going on with me and my baby's daddies. Can you believe that I even asked her for her opinion? I guess I asked her because we are so much alike. I am truly my momma's child and she's my best friend – I think. Anyway, we look so much alike except that now that she's a little older she has a little pouch around her tummy and her tits sag a little lower than mine.

Even with her tits hanging low, we are both still hammers. It didn't surprise me at all when momma said to me that I shouldn't worry about things and to just tell Roc that this is his baby and be done with it. Steering me towards the dark skinned guy is just like her. I remember when I was about fourteen or so. Somehow, I had gotten up the nerve to ask momma about this man that she was dating.

My momma is not the easiest person to talk to. When I was a kid, most of the time I just sat back and watched her do what she did and guessed why she did it. So you see I was being really brave when I asked her about her business.

"Momma why did you go out with that man last night? He wasn't cute," I asked sincerely wanting to know. Even my fourteen year old eyes could see that he was as ashy black and ugly as ashy black and ugly could be. He was ugly even before you took into account the two gold teeth that were surrounded by a mouthful of yellowish ones in his mouth. I don't even want to imagine what his breath must have smelled like.

"Tracie when you get older you'll understand about men," momma replied in a caring voice that one would expect to come from a loving mother.

"Well when I turn sixteen I'm only gonna date rich light skinned guys," I said matter of factly making sure that she knew that I remembered her rule that I couldn't date until I was sixteen.

My reply hit a nerve. My mom's entire disposition changed and she started reading me.

"Shut the hell up girl! You're talking non-sense! Don't you know that those light skin guys – the ones that you think are so fine – don't want to do nothing but get some then break your little ass heart?" I didn't understand what momma was talking about but that didn't stop her from reading me some more.

"All that pretty boy knows how to do is take and take from you. He'll get up inside of you and take all of your little stuff and then try to steal your heart so that no one can have it," she just kept right on reading me.

"Now men like I date – the ones that you think are ugly – they are just too happy to be with a woman with all of this." Momma said that with pride while running her hands over her breast, across her then flat stomach, and over her hips.

Knowing not to interrupt momma when she was like this, I just let her continue.

"Yea, a man like that is willing to give and give so that this doesn't get away from him. It's the power of a woman's pus…I mean cat. Don't forget that girl."

By this time, momma had stooped down in front of me and had both of her hands grasping my shoulders. Her deep black eyes peered directly into my eyes as if they could see right through me.

The look on my face and in my eyes had to reveal that I was clueless at the time as to what momma was getting at. All I remember thinking at the time was that I wasn't going to need any man to take care of me so I would be able to date anybody that I wanted to. What a laugh. One way or another us women are always waiting for some man. If I had only understood then what momma was talking about I would be OK now.

What I do know for sure is that I don't want this baby to be Roc's. I want it to be Len's baby. Needless to say, I ain't studying what momma is talking about. I done told Len that this is his baby and I did my best to convince him too; even if I'm not too sure myself.

Oh please God let this baby come out light or at least brown. OK-OK! I'ma just be still for a second or two and get myself together. I'm OK; I'm OK. It's just a few more days and it will be my due date and all of this will be over. I just know that Len and I are going to live happily ever after.

Tracie laid down on her living room couch and closed her eyes and drifted off to sleep. It was the first real peaceful sleep that she had in months.

Tracie woke from a deep sleep reeling from the effects of a sharp pain centered in her lower abdomen. She had never felt anything like that pain before. All she could think about was calling Len and telling him that his baby was on the way. After glancing at the clock that said a few minutes after twelve, Tracie just sat on the couch and dumbfoundly debated and rehearsed calling Len. Her next labor pain cleared her head of those thoughts and focused her on calling somebody that she knew would be there for her.

Tracie fumbled with the phone in the dark of her apartment and finally was able to push the numbers 1 and 2 to speed dial her momma.

"Momma," Tracie calmly spoke into the phone. "It's that time ... I know it's early. I guess nature is on its own time … Yes I'm sure momma! … Damn it. Why are you asking me all of these questions? … Yes my water broke and the pain is unbearable can you just get here momma … OK I'll see you when you get here."

———————————

During the short car ride to Cook County Hospital from her South Commons apartment, Tracie tried to call Len. She tried him at his house and on his cell phone. She couldn't get him. Ms. Brown had already pulled up to the emergency room door and ran to get a wheel chair before Tracie realized that they had made it to the hospital. The next contraction doubled Tracie over.

"Come on girl scoot over and get into this wheel chair," Ms. Brown urged.

"No momma. I'm not having no baby without Len being here," Tracie said softly but defiantly recovering slightly from the contraction. She pushed the phone's redial button for the umpteenth time.

"Come on girl! That baby ain't going to wait for no hardhead," Ms. Brown asserted her will.

"Momma I'm not getting out of this car until I reach him."

"Give me that damn phone girl! I'll make sure he gets here," Ms. Brown demanded.

In Tracie's eyes her mother was a giant. If she said she was going to do something then Tracie knew that it was as good as done.

"Are these his numbers?" Ms. Brown asked while scrolling down Tracie's phone call history and spotted Len's name repeated time after time on the phone's display.

"Yes, those are them," Tracie responded. "OK Mamma
I'm ready," Tracie demurely said hurriedly now hoping for relief before another pain hit. All of her pretenses of being tough were gone. Her momma was on the job. Tracie relaxed.

Tracie moved from the car's front passenger seat into the wheel chair that stood by the car with great effort. Moments later she was under a doctor's care.

With half of her job over, Ms Brown turned to her other task. Reviewing Tracie's phone settings, like any diva working a man would, she noticed that Tracie had her cell number blocked for outgoing calls.

CHAPTER 5

LEN

Len heard his home and mobile phones ringing off the hook for the last half hour. As a rule, he didn't answer the phone for blocked numbers; especially at twelve thirty at night. He let the phone go unanswered. Now, the phone was blowing up again and this time it was Tracie's number displayed on the phone's caller ID.

"Hell…"

"Len Edwards?" Ms. Brown inquired not letting Len finish saying hello. "Didn't you see Tracie trying to call you boy?" Ms. Brown screamed into the phone.

"Uh; excuse me. Who is this?" Len was finally able to get a word in edgewise.

"Forget that excuse me shit boy! This is Tracie's mother Ms. Brown! Tracie is at the hospital in labor having your baby!"

"What?"

"Fuck that what shit too! What in the hell are you going to do? You gonna be a daddy or what?" Ms. Brown spoke loud and fast wanting to get to her point and get finished with this conversation so that she could get back into the hospital and see about her own baby, Tracie.

"Uh; I don't know," Len answered honestly.

"Listen – you son of a bitch – don't have me come and get your high yellow ass. I've already told Tracie that you're on your way here and you're not gonna make a liar out of me!" Len, almost speechless and taken by surprise by the brashness of Ms. Brown, was barely able to force the words "Uh-huh" out of his mouth.

"She's at Cook County Hospital," Ms. Brown shouted into the phone loud enough for two people passing by to turn her way and look at her.

Len didn't say a word.

"Did you hear me mother fucker? I'm not playing with you!"

"Yes; Yes I hear you!"

"Good then get your ass down here now!"

Not allowing Len to answer, Ms. Brown clicked the end button on the phone. She felt internal satisfaction because of her job well done as she walked back into the hospital.

————————————

Len heard Ms. Brown loud and clear. However, he was still unclear as to what he was going to do. He thought back at all the times that he had talked to Tracie about the baby she was having over the last six months. It seemed to him that he had talked to her until he was blue in the face. None of it helped; Len couldn't get out of his mind that Tracie was trying to trap him.

It seemed to him that all of his life that somebody wanted something from him. He allowed his mind to drift to his mother who was always in need of something. She was always comparing him to a father he did not know or a brother that he didn't like. To Len, it was as if his mother wanted him to change the skin he was in. Thinking about it all now, it seems that his mother was the worst one of them all.

He had to get his mind off of his family and back onto his dilemma with Tracie. For some reason, for the past few days every time he started thinking about Tracie and the baby, he would wind up having deep thoughts about his mother and brother. It was all messing with his head.

I've always loved my mother. Hell, if it wasn't for her I wouldn't even be here. Am I right? The bad thing about it all is that no matter how hard I try to please her, it seems as if she thinks that I owe more. It was hard but I had to put her on the back burner or risk losing myself. As early as I can remember, I have been in my own little world. I don't have no father; at least not one that I know of. When I asked Us-Ma about him, all she would ever say is, "That mother fucker; I don't know where he is! Why you asking about him? He don't want your ass."

It wasn't what she said about a father I didn't know; it was how she said it. There was an edge of hate in her voice that was evident. It was the same voice that she would use when she was talking to me after she had been drinking. She would be mad at me for some reason or another and say something like, "Look at you looking like your jackass father. He wasn't nothing and neither are you."

The distain in her voice was heart breaking. It wasn't long before I stopped missing what I didn't have and just went deeper into my mental shell. Oh yea! When I was little, I had a shell that protected me from everything – I wish I had that protection now.

Before things became really bad at home, I really looked up to my older brother Maurice. For some reason he had Us-Ma all figured out. He could do no wrong. It was the tie that bound us together. Me, on the other hand I couldn't do anything right when it came to pleasing Us-Ma when I was a kid. The house was never clean enough, the clothes that I washed were never folded right. Nothing ever was right except that my grades in school were always good. School work just came natural for me.

As good as my grades were in school my behavior in school was twice as bad. For a while there, my teachers were sending note after note home to Us-Ma complaining about my shenanigans at school. If I wasn't talking and disrupting the class then I was shooting spitballs at somebody. I had an array of tricks that included passing notes in class, fighting other kids, and talking back to the teacher.

None of my offenses in school compared to the trouble that I got into when I went up this fine little girl's skirt in the fourth grade. I think I did it just because she thought that I wouldn't do it.

Early during the school day, I had peeped out from across the room that the little girl had on red panties. I couldn't miss them because she was sitting all wide legged and all across from me in class. Our desks were arranged in an oval pattern around the classroom. I wasn't really trying to see between her legs but her knees were so wide apart and the red of her drawers reflected brightly off her cream colored legs. I couldn't help but see.

What was a mischievous fourth grader to do sitting there bored out of his mind listening to the never ending drawl of a battle ax of a teacher? Needless to say, I had to write a note about those underwear and pass it around the class. Before too long and before the little girl had a chance to correct her leg position, the attention of half of the boys in the class was focused between the girl's legs.

Later on that day at recess, it was on. I don't know who tricked on me but someone did because that girl knew that I was the one who wrote the note about her. A verbal altercation started first.

"Why you write that note about me Len?" The red underwear girl demanded to know. She was closing fast into my personal space with a group of kids close behind her.

Somehow, kids always can smell a school yard fight about to happen and are attracted to it like flies to shit.

"I on't know," I said hunching my shoulders. The red underwear girl recently had a growth spurt and stood a head taller than me.

"What you doing looking under my dress?"

"You had your legs all open like you wanted me to look," I retorted with the cockiness of a fourth grader.

"You're just nasty Len Edwards! You just mad because don't nobody want your stank ass."

"You better get out my face girl!"

"I might have on red underwear but you won't ever touch them," the red underwear girl taunted.

She was doing her best to humiliate me in front of the whole school yard. I lost it. Before I knew what I was doing I had grabbed the girl and was raising her skirt up so that everybody could see those red drawers. I did it just in time for the gym teacher to see what I did.

I was busted. Caught by the one teacher that every kid in the whole school was afraid of; Mr. Powers. I was going to get the paddle for sure. It was a big paddle that had half inch holes drilled into it. The holes allowed the air to hiss through them as the paddle was coming towards your behind. When the paddle made contact with your body, your skin was sucked through the holes in the paddle causing extreme pain. Just thinking about it now, I can feel the pain.

As if ten swats from Mr. Powers wasn't enough punishment, they called Us-Ma too. I guess the phone call pushed her over the top. She had had enough and was fed up with me. In what seemed like seconds of her getting the phone call from the school, Us-Ma was there with an extension cord in her hand.

While she was beating the hell out of me, I didn't scream out because I knew that the entire class would hear. It didn't matter because Mrs. Hayes, my old battle axe of a teacher, was out in the hallway screaming at the top of her lungs for Us-Ma to stop beating the shit out of me. In no time, the hallway was filled with teachers seeing what the commotion was all about. Some brave kids came out to see what was going on only to be shoed back into the classroom by the teachers. It was an ugly sight. All I could do is wrap myself into a ball to try and make myself small until the beating was over.

It finally stopped. A lot of big red welts, some broken skin, but I would live. It was over but I would never be the same. It was one thing to get beat down at home but another thing entirely to have it happen in public in front of all the rest of the kids at school. The shell around me got a little thicker that day. Can you believe that three months later Us-Ma still remembered what I had done and I had a Christmas with no gifts? I guess I deserved it.

After a three-day suspension, when I came back to school, my behavior didn't change but the teacher's tolerance of it had after seeing Us-Ma in action. Mrs. Hayes started giving me what I now know was special attention. At the time, it just seemed like punishment.

She routinely kept me after school to clean the chalkboards or some other task. While I was there alone with her, she would talk to me. The one thing that she said repeatedly that stuck with me through all my school days was that I could be anything that I wanted to be if I would just study hard and try.

She saw to it that I did the studying hard that year that she was my teacher. She gave me extra work and books to read and she would take time to teach me little tricks when it came to doing math. After that year, for the next four years until I graduated from eight grade, she would always find me in the school yard or in class and give me books that she knew that I would like or ask me to come and help her after school.

By the time that eighth grade graduation rolled around, can you believe that Mrs. Hayes even stopped looking like a battle-axe? I think she had to be about fifty at the time but her age just disappeared from her after awhile. I remember at graduation she was so happy to see me graduating. She hugged me and told me to always do my best. I said I would. I'll never forget her hug. It was my first one from any woman. She felt so soft I could have stayed there forever.

I think that it was that hug that flipped a switch inside of me. Within two months of graduation, my voice changed from a childish squeak to a rich manly baritone. Before thirteen set in good, a fine, well-defined mustache developed over my upper lip. I also grew about a foot in height and my shoe size went from a size seven to a size ten and growing.

My mother's friend Cat – I have no idea what her real name is – noticed me changing too. Over the years, since I was about nine years old, I would spend time over to Ms. Cat's house helping out with little odd jobs. Most of the time she would have jobs for me when Us-Ma was in a mood to kill me for some reason or another.

Ms. Cat's family owned a two flat building on Wells Street. With most people in the neighborhood living in the projects, many thought that Ms. Cat's family was high class. To me, she was just my mother's sweet and pretty friend who stayed on the top floor of the building by herself. With a building, there was always something that needed to be done so there was never a shortage of work around the place. No one raised an eyebrow when on a ninety-five degree August day Ms. Cat asked if I could come over to her place and move her refrigerator and stove so that she could clean behind them.

After I moved the appliances, cleaned behind them, and put them back in place, I did what I had been doing for years after I had done work at Ms. Cat's house. Under the comfort of an old box fan, I settled down on her front room leopard print couch, turned on her Sony Trinitron TV, and relaxed. Just as an old episode of "*Good Times*" was heating up, Ms. Cat called for me to come into her room.

"Do you see anything that you want?" Ms. Cat sweetly asked just as I arrived at her bedroom door.

My eyes were bucking out of my head looking at her sitting on the edge of her bed, legs open showing me my future, wearing only a black lacy bra and matching panties. Instinctively, my hand reached down to my dick to see what was wrong with it; it was throbbing so hard.

It was whopping hard standing straight up extending up to my belly button. I didn't know what to do with it; it was just there. I was speechless.

"Come here and let Cat see if she can fix that," she growled. Her eyes were fixed on my hand covering the bulge in my pants and her mouth was showing a mouthful of teeth; almost too many for her smallish mouth. It seemed her teeth were ready to bite.

Like a little puppy, I did just as I was told. When I got in front of her, I just stood there not believing how beautiful she was. She was always pretty to me but right then; damn she was gorgeous. She stood about five one or two with caramel colored skin that contrasted perfectly with the black lace that covered exactly enough to make her skin sexy. Her short jet black hair was tossed about her head recklessly revealing a wild aggressive nature that was hidden to me before now.

I wanted to be eaten by Ms. Cat. Her big deep brown expressive eyes, that were almost circular, continued to talk to me long after her words had stopped ringing in my ear. "Come here and let Cat see if she can fix that." She grabbed and tugged my dick once through my pants and it was over. In ecstasy, I vibrated in her hand for what seemed like an eternity. I didn't know why but I was slightly embarrassed when I had finally finished.

"That was strong. Lets get you cleaned up. Okay?" Ms. Cat offered.

I still was speechless but I wanted anything that she wanted. I didn't have a mind as she led me to the bathroom.

The bathroom was filled with candles that were already lit. The bathroom was roomy and beautiful with the oversized soaker bathtub that was large enough to accommodate three.

Gaining my bearings, I reached out to Ms. Cat in an effort to touch her for the first time. My hand grasped one of her breast tentatively. Ms. Cat just smiled at me and continued to remove my shirt.

"Whooo! That's what I'm talking about," she said getting my shirt off, rubbing the flat of her hands over my chest drawing her body closer to me. "I'ma take good care of you," hissed out of her mouth like a viper stalking prey.

I didn't know anything else to do but smile. I loved the attention and stood there in anticipation. Ms. Cat began to run bath water adding a little bit of this and a little bit of that to the water. When the tub was a little less than half full she finished undressing me and told me to get into the tepid bath water that was topped with foam.

"Aren't you getting in with me," I asked knowing what I wanted for the first time since this started.

"Hey! I'm in charge here. We'll get there. I've got some work to put in first."

I didn't understand what she was talking about; all this was new to me. I just laid back into the water and cleared my mind. I was used to a woman being in charge so I saw no reason not to relent to her.

Ms. Cat sat on the side of the tub and took one of my feet in her hand. Expertly, she took her time and gave me a pedicure. She rubbed and nurtured my feet like they belonged to a Greek god. She took her time. Every time the water began to loose its heat she would run a little hot water into the tub to warm the water up. When she took one of my feet into her mouth and raked her teeth over its sole, I was in heaven. At that moment, I didn't need anything else; my shell was washed away.

Next was a full body massage that started with my legs. I was rock hard again.

"I haven't forgotten about him; we'll get to that after awhile," she said while popping my dick hard with her finger causing my hard-on to instantly dwindle. "Isn't this better than sex?"

I had no idea how to answer. It was all sex to me. When she finished with the massage, I was more relaxed than I think I have ever been. By this time, the water was high in the tub and I sat there wondering what was next. She didn't disappoint. With the candles flickering off of her reflective skin, she slowly removed her bra and panties.

The hair between her thighs was long but neat and it called to me first. I lightly touched it. Seeing where my interest lied, Cat whispered in a raspy voice, "I don't like fingers inside of me."

She lightly grasped my hand – it didn't take much to move me; I was under her control – and guided it teaching it how to touch and provide pleasure. Her eyes were closed and all I heard her say was "umh" a few times as her hips swayed slightly.

After a few seconds of letting me touch her, she stepped up into the tub with me and began guiding my hands showing me how to wash, rub and caress her. I was a quick study. When she noticed that I was too excited she would do her finger trick to make it go down saying, "I'm not ready for him yet." I learned a lot in that tub but it was nothing compared to what she taught me in her bed-room afterwards.

Getting out of the tub, you could feel the clamminess of the muggy Chicago night that still held a temperature around ninety.

In her bed, drenched with sweat from the banging of two well toned bodies together, I needed relief. She went in the kitchen and retrieved a container of ice, a bowl of peach Jell-O, and some grapes to cool us off. Eating Jell-O off of a warm body is much sweeter than eating it from a spoon. When she put Jell-O between her legs on her cat I was hesitant. I had always heard stories about that and didn't really want to go there.

Everything else that night was good and I felt obligated so I slurped the Jell-O up with my eyes looking into hers to see if I was doing what she wanted me to do. Looking down at me she was already smiling. She smeared some more of the Jell-O between her legs and nodded to me.

I wanted to give so I started licking and sucking the treat. While I was doing my thing she was telling me what felt good, where to linger, and what she didn't like with her fingers on the top of my head. I learned more in that short time about a woman than I have ever learned since.

Hours later, spent and worn, Ms. Cat began to talk to me and educate me.

"This is only between us. Don't you dare tell anybody. Okay?

"Okay," I said in my recently acquired rich voice. I was even beginning to sound like a man to myself.

"Now you watch yourself out there. You can't be giving all those girls out there what you gave me." I just smiled.

"You are such a pretty boy. I mean man. Those girls out there are going to try to turn you out."

"No they're not. I'm only gonna do what I want to do," I assured her and myself. Thinking about it now I can only laugh at how naive I really was.

I never had any more Ms. Cat after that night. I guess she got what she wanted.

––––––––––––––––––

Up until I was about fourteen, Maurice and I acted like brothers should act towards one anther; I think. I mean it was never all for one and one for all between us but until then I really did look up to him and wanted to be like him. I admired how things came so easy for him. It seemed that everything came so hard for me.

I first noticed a rift between us after I was big enough to play sports with him. Maurice would always want to compete with me. All I wanted to do was hangout and have fun. When we would play softball or basketball we always were on separate teams. If somehow we wound up on the same team, it wouldn't be too long before

Maurice would quit the game, go home, and take his ball with him. Back then, I thought that I must have been doing something wrong for my brother to be like that.

My shell of insecurity got just that much thicker. You know, even then my shell didn't stop me from looking up to him though.

Looking up to and having any kind of close brotherhood with Maurice ended all at once over an incident with a girl. The girl's name was Princess. She was flat out a beautiful girl. I was about fourteen and she was probably a few years older than I was but we had a lot in common. We would talk for hours in the park, our building's courtyard, or outside of her apartment. The tie that bound us together was that both of our mothers were overbearing. We used each other as a means of escape.

Princess and I would talk about our dreams. I remember she was going to be a nurse and I was going to be a doctor. For hours on end we would sit letting our imaginations run wild out loud to each other. So naturally, when I couldn't tell Maurice about my experience with Ms. Cat, I turned to Princess. Princess was different from everybody else; we were so comfortable with each other I could tell her anything. I told her every detail about my afternoon and night with Ms. Cat.

After I told Princess about my Ms. Cat story she entrusted me with a secret about her. Her moms was dressing her up at night and sending her out into the night or to different men's places. After her momma found out that she had sex with some boy she said, "If you're gonna give it up you might as well make us some money with it."

It didn't seem like she was upset about what her momma had her doing or anything. She just told me like it was natural and just a fact of life.

"Do you like doing that," I asked Princess unsure how I should feel about her revelation since she seemed to be okay with it.

"No not really. I would rather be with you," she replied with a smile and a half giggle.

"What do you mean?" I asked unsure what she was driving at.

"You know. You can show me what Ms. Cat showed you." She smiled as she told me her intentions and then leaned closer to me and gave me a kiss on the cheek.

The very thin shell that I needed to protect me when I was with her faded. I didn't know how to say no. Not

completely out of my mind, I did have sense enough to
let her know that Maurice was at home.

Her response of "I on't care " to my brothers
presence started us to walking down the building's
balcony towards the apartment. I demurely walked a few
paces behind her. By the time that we reached the
apartment door I was excited. Entering the apartment, I
was confronted by Maurice.

"Man Princess wants to um; you know. I mean it's
on; you want to hang?" I quietly asked my voice just above
a whisper.

"I'm telling Us-Ma!" Was all that came out of his
mouth. He said it loud and sternly. I was blown away by
what he said. In my excitement walking down the
balcony, I forgot to put my protective shell back around
me. In utter disbelief of the words that came out of my
brother's mouth, my shell immediately reformed and
then thickened around me. After that, I didn't hear
anything else that Maurice said. The words "I'm telling
Us-Ma" were ringing in my ears blocking out everything
else that was being said in the room.

I became small. I just couldn't take anymore mental
body blows from my own brother. Recovering a little
from the mental body blow, I saw Maurice and Princess
drinking Us-Ma's Old Grand Dad with some grape Kool
– Aid.

*Wait a second! Princess is supposed to be my friend
and what the hell are they doing drinking Us-Ma's
stuff?* I thought to myself. You know that you don't
mess with Us-Ma's stuff unless you're looking for a
beat down. *For that matter what is Maurice doing*

drinking at all? I continued to think. I had never seen Maurice drink any alcohol before.

I put all of those thoughts out of my mind, made myself still smaller, and left the apartment so that they could do their thing in peace.

The next day, by mistake, I ran into Princess sitting in our building's courtyard. As soon as I saw her sitting on the top rail of the courtyard bench, I turned to walk away. It was too late; she saw me and called out.

"Hey Len! Wait up."

I heard her but I didn't turn around; I just kept right on walking as if I didn't hear her calling my name. It didn't matter because a few moments later she caught up to me. "Len your brother don't know shit about sex," she said with a snicker in her voice.

"What you talking about girl," I replied defensively after being caught off guard by her remark.

"I mean all he knew how to do was sit there like a dummy. I tried to show him something but he was the worst trick I've ever had," she said hunching her shoulders in disbelief.

"Look Princess, my brother ain't no trick," I replied with an edge to my voice!

"Well he gave me twenty dollars; I think that makes him a trick." Princess was outright laughing now. I was hurt again. My friend – the person that I told some of my deepest thoughts – was laughing at me and my family. This time I didn't get small. I busted out of my shell.

"I don't know nothing about no trick stuff!" I replied with authority. "All I know is that I would break that back."

"So you think that you're that good huh?" Princess slyly questioned.

I was too inexperienced then but I know now that all she was doing with me was putting some work in. She already knew what she wanted. She was doing what she was doing not because of anything I said, but because she wanted to. It was the first time, in a whole line of times, that I thought I was doing the fucking just to be fucked in the end. All I was to her was a new dick. Over the years, I've learned the hard way that there's very little love between men and women. There's a lot of status taking, economic exchanges, and lustful unions but very little love.

By the time that we got to the apartment, I was ready to show this girl a thing or two. I busted through the door of the apartment and Maurice came out of the back. The shit eating grin on his face let me know that he thought that his number was up again. I didn't confront him and before I knew it he was out in the front room offering up Kool-Aid and Old Grand Dad like he did the day before. Princess drank up the drink and then told Maurice to get lost that she had something that she wanted to show me.

If looks could kill, I would have been dead from the look that Maurice shot me as he left the room. I didn't have a shell around me and I didn't care what anybody thought right then. I was on a mission to show this girl that I could go.

I looked at Princess in a different light now. I sat back on the couch and in a low voice called Princess over to me. She played her part well. She came over and bent over at the waist acting like she had something to pickup and showed me her white panties riding high on her cheeks.

The only way that I controlled myself was to remember what Ms. Cat said about putting some work in.

"Girl you've got to put some work in to get some of this," I said to her in a low voice as she looked over her shoulder to assess the effect that her little move of bending over showing me some draws was having on me.

"I ain't afraid of you Len," she said turning around, coming closer to me, facing me, and hopping up on my lap straddling her legs over mine.

She started undressing herself and me. I just closed my eyes and imagined that she was Ms. Cat. When I finally opened my eyes again, Us-Ma was standing over us with a broomstick and an iron.

I know that Maurice could hear her coming because Us-Ma had a habit of jingling her keys before she unlocked the door. I think that she did it just to give us a little advance warning that she was coming through the door. No, my brother let me get caught with my pants down.

Us-Ma beat me and Princess like we were slaves. Princess ran out the house with no clothes on before Us-Ma could get her good. Me, Us-Ma beat me until she couldn't lift her arms anymore. A week after that beating I still had bruises and scabs. You know what? I still got a few scars on my back and arms from that beating.

The whipping was nothing – I was used to those – what hurt the most was being on punishment the next month and hearing Us-Ma and Maurice out in the front room having a good ole time like I wasn't even there. I changed after that. I obtained a new industrial strength shell that could withstand almost anything. My shell has only been completely down a few times after that. With Kayla, with Tracie, and with my best friend Dee. After opening up the shell and things not working out, I think I might be lonely forever.

Len knew that he had to get himself together and get to that hospital. Five minutes had passed since Ms. Brown's call but he still wasn't mentally ready to handle things. Trying to concentrate on what he had to do wasn't working; Len was mentally back in his past again.

I have been working like a man since I was sixteen. Nobody was taking care of me so I had to work to take care of myself. Us-Ma did provide the basics but more times than I care to remember, I went to school in some of Maurice's holey hand me downs. It's hard on you when kids make fun of your gear all the time at school. I remember one time some girls walking up behind me in the school hallway singing "Skin Tight" because my out of fashion pants were so tight. Those were some hard times.

While I was working, I didn't let my school work slip. I was already ahead of where I should have been in school because of all the years that Us-Ma made me help Maurice with his school work. It's good that I learned something from it because Maurice sure isn't using anything that he learned in school with his alcohol and drug problems kicking him in the ass. I don't think that he has had a sober day since I saw him drinking with Princess.

Maurice and I aren't even friends now let alone brotherly towards one another. It just wasn't in the cards for us. It didn't matter much. By the time that I left for college I was totally emancipated from both Maurice and Us-Ma.

Life on my own, with no one taking my hard earned money from me to buy Old Grand Dad or cigarettes, was fine with me. I always hid my money at home ever since Us-Ma took my paper route money one year and drank and smoked it up. I had to hide that money good because

Maurice had a growing monkey on his back that Us-Ma didn't want to see. Arriving at Northern, I met my best friend Dee on my second day there. He was truly my brother in all of his actions. Dee and I ran all the girls so I didn't need anybody else to hang out with. Between Dee and the girls at Northern I was all right. You wouldn't even know that I had a shell at all.

There were short girls, fat girls, and tall girls. They came in all shapes, sizes, and colors. There were even a few White, Asian, Middle Eastern, and Hispanic girls too.

I quickly learned to like the girls that liked me. It's easier to like them than to try to make someone not interested in you like you. They were good and many of them got under my shell for a little while but none of them could make it go away or keep it from coming back. You know what though, all of that sex did kind of turn me out.

By the time that I had pledged Alpha – I pledged because my boy Dee wanted to – I knew that each time that I had sex with a different girl that my reputation was on the line. It became like a business. I didn't need any more male friends. All they ever wanted to do was get in

your business and try to get a woman off of your rep. I
had over fifty Alpha brothers on the yard but still only hung
out with my best friend Dee. Who needs more than one
friend anyway.

————————————————

For a short while my last girlfriend Kayla had my
number. My best friend Dee had died and Kayla was
there filling in the voids in my life. I let my shell
dissipate when it came to her and lost my mind. She was
my everything. What I didn't know until it was too late
was that I wasn't her everything. Kayla was the type of
woman that loves her freedom and has learned over the
years how to hold her own in all situations.

Up until then I was used to dealing with women who
had the other woman syndrome and approach to men.
Women who specialize in holding a man and telling him
that everything is alright even when she knows that it's
not. The type of woman who tells you that you're right
even when she knows that you're wrong. The type of
woman that freely wraps her body around yours and
wicks away all of the hurt from you when you can take
no more hurt. I guess all of my other girl friends before
Kayla were acting like the other woman. They loved
quick, deep, and hard; it was their job.

Expertly they filled and fulfilled those vacant spots
that a wife or a steady girlfriend might have forgotten
existed. All of them were fulfilling the role of the other
woman.

Kayla was different. When someone is trying to love
you forever, they tell you like it is. They don't sugar
coat things. Sometimes they forget that your ego might
not be able to handle the truth. What they offer you is
priceless and just like fine china, if you don't treat what
they give with care, it will break on you. Once it is

broken, for whatever reason, the masterpiece that was being created will never be what it could have been.

Kayla wasn't taking second best. She dropped me hard and I didn't even see it coming. And when the bottom dropped out of our relationship it broke me into two.

To make matters worse, about a year later when I found out that Kayla was dating someone else – someone that I knew too – I did the unthinkable. Since then I've asked GOD to forgive me for doing what I had to do and I think that he has. I don't think about what I did too much; that's how I get by.

After Kayla, being spiteful and trying to get even with someone I had already did my worst to, I started dating Tracie. I did everything to make her fall for me. Flowers, calls in the middle of the night and endless sex. Like I said, I was on a mission. How in the hell could I have known that a woman who I had no intentions with, who I thought was so far below my league, would get next to me. Clearly she did get to me.

Tracie pulled me back from a dark place. A place where no man wants or needs to be. In love; I mean in lust with a woman who doesn't want you. It was the worst feeling in the world and drove me to commit moral sins. In the end, all of the sex in the world wasn't enough to satisfy me. I was truly a son of a bitch towards women.

I can't even count how many women I went through after Kayla and before I started dating Tracie. I don't even want to think about it. When I was doing it, I didn't care. Sex was free and while I was having it I felt fulfilled. After I was finished with one, no matter how good she was, I was still longing for something – none of them did it for me. Like I said I was truly a son of a bitch.

I was still that same son of a bitch when I decided to try a little taste of Tracie. I came on to her out of spite. I knew that she had slept with Al and that Al had been Kayla's lover after me. It wasn't as if Al hadn't already paid for what he did to me. My dating Tracie was just frosting on the cake. I really didn't want her – I mean she was well below my standards and in no shape, form or fashion did she fit my M.O.

I generally go for light skinned women who are soft and patient with me. Everybody that I knew was surprised that I was seeing Tracie with her being dark and not very attractive in the face. But after experiencing her I didn't need a shell anymore. We were an item.

Then it happened. About six months into our relationship, Tracie had to go and get herself knocked-up. She wasn't like a one night stand or anything so, yea, I was riding bare-back in that pussy. She said that she liked it better that way and she assured me that I didn't have anything to worry about.

Now Tracie is kind of wild but that's exactly what I needed after being turned out by so many women over the years. I needed a woman who could handle me. Tracie fit that role nicely. Tracie is as tough as nails and I like that about her. I knew that she wasn't going to break. She also always seemed to have my best interest at heart whenever we would talk.

Thinking about it now, Tracie is like a mixture of Kayla and Princess put together. Don't get me wrong, she has none of their looks, she's uncouth, and you'd never know what might come out of her mouth. Yea, my girl is truly a piece of work.

You know what? You're not going to believe this but after awhile, all the things that I didn't like about her, even her looks, became unimportant once we started clicking. That is, I got over everything except one thing. Tracie loves sex more than anybody I've ever met before. In some ways that's a good thing. It was all good at first. If there's one thing I like, it's a girl to be ready to accommodate when I need her to be ready.

Hey, I'm still only one man. If I was busy or just too worn out to have sex, Tracie would keep pressuring me for what she needed. Then, if I was still not giving it up, I would hear about it.

"I'ma have to go get me some somewhere – you know that don't cha?"

"Yea! Right girl. You know that you can't replace this," I said with confidence.

"Len you know if I can't get what I want from you then there's always somebody standing in line to give me what I need."

I thought she was joking. I mean, I was breaking that back. Besides, Tracie would keep coming at me until one way or the other she got what she wanted from me. As quiet as I kept it from her, I liked her approach. It felt good to be wanted.

About three or four months into our relationship, it all stopped. We were still having sex two or three times a day but on those rare occasions that something came up and I couldn't be around – you know a business trip or just being tired – Tracie wouldn't care about not having sex like she would before.

I saw the change in her and didn't see it at the same time. When you're in love you only see what you want to see. Those rose-colored glasses that I was wearing were a mother fucker; they shielded out more than just UV rays.

I began to question things when Tracie came up with this I'm pregnant thing. When she first told me, I was on cloud nine. Then, I started thinking about things and my mind became full of doubts. I keep thinking that this whole thing is a setup. Everything was just too perfect. My mind kept working and the next thing you know, I couldn't shake a feeling that this might not be my baby at all.

I told Tracie how I felt. Tracie just replied, "I know where my pussy has been. This is your baby Len. Come on let's not even go there."

What she said didn't matter because I was already going there. I've spent the last six months there. I stopped seeing Tracie and for the first time, since my encounter with Ms. Cat, I wasn't having sex with someone. For the last six months I have been trying to get my head together about Tracie and the baby.

About an hour went by since Ms. Brown's phone call. Len was driving one million miles per hour on the Eisenhower Expressway moving towards Cook County Hospital. Approaching the Ashland exit for the hospital, Len noticed coming up behind him an ambulance with its lights flashing and horns blaring.

By the time that the ambulance caught up to him, Len was already on the Ashland Avenue exit ramp. Always the responsible driver, he pulled to his right to allow the ambulance to pass by him.

The closer the ambulance came to his car the more he could feel a chill coming over him. As the ambulance past by, it without notice to most discharged a small essence of it's cargo. In that instant both Us-Ma and Maurice were in his car with him.

"What the fu.." Len caught his language before he actually said the word fuck. The years had not changed his respect for the presence of Us-Ma. "How did … I mean why are you guys. What's going on here?"

"Len we needed to talk to you before its too late," Maurice said in a calming voice. It was the type of voice that older brothers often use with younger siblings to calm them when they are scared.

Us-Ma's face was aglow. "Len boy you look good. I didn't do too bad did I?" Us-Ma couldn't take her eyes off Len. He was all she had left in the world. He alone would have the burden of defining her past existence on earth.

Seeing Us-Ma and Maurice made Len tense. All of the horrors that had been running through his mind just minutes before were still with him. Len reconciled that he was dreaming. This being a dream he decided not to go into a shell and just let it pass.

"This ain't no dream boy," Us-Ma replied as if she was reading his thoughts. "We're here to help. We can't stay long. You see we have passed. It's almost time for us to go away." Just then she remembered when it had been that she had felt this good before. It was when she was a newborn; just ready for the world.

Len didn't pull away from the off ramp curb. He just sat there trying to get himself together. This couldn't be happening. Could it?

Maurice placed his hand on his brother's shoulder to comfort him. His hand was weightless but he could feel its presence. The hand's coolness was comforting to Len.

"Look Len, I know that things haven't been the best between us. We have only a little while to make amends. Even though I didn't know how to show you, I was always proud of you. You handled everything with so much strength. I know life was hard; but look at you now."

"Yea! Look at me. You guys just don't know. I'm fucked up," Len replied. For the first time he was talking in earnest to his mother and brother without a shell around him.

"Watch your mouth boy! I might not be among the living but that don't mean that you can disrespect me with that type of language," Us-Ma snapped. "I can see you're still like your jackass father ain't you?"

"Len what she means is that you've got to let go of the past. There's still time for you," Maurice interjected not wanting things to get out of hand. He cut his eyes at Us- Ma letting her know how he felt about her last comment.

He realized that this was something that he should have been doing a long time ago.

Len looked over at Maurice and for the first time in ages he felt a warmth between him and his brother. The warmth he felt carried with it a cleansing that was like a burden being removed from him. Len's wide smile was all that Maurice needed to continue this exchange.

"Len I was in that ambulance coming from Cook County Jail that just went by you. I didn't make it. I'm gone."

Maurice's face looked sad. However, the remains of the hard life that he had lived were fading from his face right in front of Len's eyes. Feeling refreshed Maurice continued. "Brother, there's still time for you to enjoy life. You've got what it takes. I was always jealous at how you always grabbed life by the horns. I wish I was more like you."

"You know what? I've always wanted to be like you," Len revealed.

"All right enough of this mushy shit. I've got some stuff that I need to say too," Us-Ma interrupted.

She hasn't changed a bit, Len thought to himself. As she was talking, Len could see all of the telltale signs of the hard life that she had lived in her face.

"When you get to that hospital you make sure that you come see about me! I don't want them Taylors to handle my body. Give me to Leak. You hear me!"

She didn't wait for an answer before she was talking again. "Now make sure you invite everybody to my funeral. I mean everybody except that Cat. I'm mad at her. Oh yea. There's insurance …"

Len had stopped listening to her a few seconds ago. Len looked over at Maurice and he could see that he was now glowing, The two brothers made eye contact with each other and both at the same time hunched their shoulders in disbelief at how Us-Ma was going on and on.

Just as Len was about to open his mouth to say something to Maurice, his thoughts were interrupted by a loud tapping on his driver's side window.

"Let me see your license and insurance," the white Chicago Police sergeant demanded as Len was rolling down the car window.

"Yes sir," Len said reaching for his wallet.

The officer took the license and insurance card from Len and flashed his flash light inside of Len's car.

"Mr. Edwards what are you doing sitting out here on the off ramp?" The officer inquired while reading the license and checking the dates on the insurance card. The officer's voice revealed that he was a little hot at having to pull over and see what this car was doing on the side of the off ramp.

"I was just sitting here talking to my mother and my brother officer." Len looked around the car but there was no one there.

The officer made and assumption and replied, "This isn't where you stop and talk on the cell phone you idiot."

"Yes sir," Len replied letting the cop's idiot remark slide. Len had tears welling up in his eyes. He didn't want to explain the impossible to the officer. It was enough that he knew that it was true. The pain of his loss was beginning to set in as a tear rolled down his cheek before he could catch it and wipe it away.

"All right. Move along sir. Move along," The officer demanded handing Len back his license and insurance card.

———————————

Len made it to the hospital parking lot and could go no farther. He spent the next two hours in the car talking with himself after calling the hospital and confirming that Maurice and Us-Ma had both actually died. After a while, he was able to pull himself together. Finally, almost five hours after receiving Ms. Brown's phone call, Len walked through the door of the hospital.

Len stood outside of Tracie's room still not knowing what to do. His mind was twisted; he wanted to believe Tracie Inside of himself he had already reconciled that he could be a great father. If it was in a book he would read it. If it could be taught he would learn it. Nothing would be more important than his child.

Len entered the room. Tracie lay in her bed sleep. Len was surprised to see the newborn baby that Tracie had given birth to also asleep in a small crib next to Tracie's bed.

The baby was a beautiful walnut color. Her color contrasted perfectly with the pink bedding she was wrapped in. Len couldn't help himself. He reached out and engulfed the little four pound six ounce baby girl into his massive arms. She just laid sleep in his arms safe and secure. While holding her something happen deep inside of him.

For the first time in his life, Len felt truly settled. He felt that his destiny was taking shape. For the first time he understood what his best friend Dee meant when he said that his grandfather had told him that he would know that it was time to settle down when there was nothing more important to him than his family.

Empowered, Len exhaled deeply expelling his past. Ready for the future, Len began in a tone and volume that was only intended for God's and little Len's ears – *that's it your name is going to be Lyn,* Len thought to himself.

"My heavenly father; I know that I have not proven myself fit to travel this road. I ask that you forgive my past and guide Lyn, Tracie, and my future. I ask these things in your Son's name. Amen."

Len gently laid the baby that he had taken the liberty of naming Lyn back into her crib carefully supporting her head and body while he did so. His huge hands had never been so gentle. Not wanting to be separated from her, Len let his hands linger at her toes touching each one of them one by one through her little footies. "This one has my heart," Len softly spoke to himself.

Len knew that his heart was vulnerable. He knew that the only way that he could protect it was to be the best man that he could be. Needing to talk to Tracie to explain what he was feeling, Len turned to Tracie and spoke to her sleeping body.

"Tracie we need to talk."

At that precise moment Len understood that there was really nothing that needed to be talked about. Under these circumstances action was worth a million times more than all of the thoughts in his head.

"Excuse me nurse. My name is Len Edwards and Tracie Brown's baby is my baby," I said with my chest held out.

"Well alrighty then," I remember the nurse smartly replying.

"Can you tell me how to get to the office to sign the papers to admit that the baby is mine?" I asked wanting to get the ball rolling as soon as possible.

"You don't have to go anywhere. The social worker is due to be on the ward at nine. Mr. Edward's that is when normal visiting hours are."

The nurse had to remind me that they had made an exception for me to be on the floor at this time of the morning.

"OK. But can you do me a small favor?" I requested.

"What is it that you need young man?"

"I have a few very important errands to run. If the girls wake-up can you let them know that I was here and that I'll be back as soon as visiting hours start?" Len sincerely asked.

"That'll be no problem. I'll be here until ten and I'll let them know when they wake-up."

"Thanks." I said and scurried to the elevator.

Len took the time that he had and went and saw Us-Ma and Maurice. There it became all too real to him that they were really gone. The morgue attendant was very helpful in getting things situated. Leak did a brisk business with the county so the morgue attendant had their phone number handy.

After finishing up at the morgue, Len drove home still under the baby's spell. At his Oak Park apartment, Len quickly did the shit, shower, and shave thing. He was back in his car by seven forty-two. Driving again, he didn't feel any of the effects from being up all the night before. Len was on a natural high.

Understanding that a father needs a job, Len while driving used his cell phone to call his job at Brainstorm Advertising. It was still before eight – the time that the company's receptionist and phone operator came in – so he had to navigate through a maze of phone menus to get to his boss's voice mail. Through his voice mail message to his boss, Len requested two days off from work.

The message he left for his boss was detailed enough to require Len to redial the office number three times after running out of time in the mailbox. He outlined the history and current status of all of the open projects that he was working on. He let his boss know the projects that would need attention while he was away and how he proposed to stay on top of them in his absence. He summarized the message that he left by saying that he was sure that his absence for the two days would not affect any of his project deadlines. Lastly, he left his cell phone number to be used in case anything came up that he didn't cover in his message.

The phone message that Len left showed a level of maturity and caring that he had not displayed before at work. The phone call out of the way, Len turned the engine of his two door convertible three series BMW over, put the car in drive, and pulled out of his apartment's driveway. Len loved his little black BMW but that didn't stop him from entertaining thoughts of trading it in for a less expensive family four door; probably something American but definitely not a mini-van. *I can't go there,* Len thought to himself.

Len checked the time again; he didn't want to be late getting back to the hospital. It was just a few minutes after eight. The thought, *I still have plenty of time to get some flowers*, raced through his head. Now headed to Blossoms of Hawaii, a south Michigan Avenue florist, Len took time and turned his attention to getting his mother and brother settled.

He dialed the phone number to Leak Funeral Home.

After about five rings of the phone, a morbid sounding voice said, "Hello; Leak Funeral Home. May I help you?"

The entire conversation didn't take long. In less than five minutes the voice had efficiently ascertained the deceases' names, the hospital they were in, who was going to be responsible for payment, and a credit card number to charge initial fees related to pickup. Len set an afternoon time frame to meet with the funeral director after the bodies were picked up.

Task finished, Len continued on his way to the florist. Blossoms of Hawaii, Len spent one hundred eighty dollars on two floral arrangements – one very large one and one small one for the baby. The large arrangement was so big that Len had to let the convertible top down on his car to fit the package of flowers into the car.

Pulling away from the flower shop, Len checked the time once again. *It's just a little after eight thirty; I can still take the side street and be on time,* Len thought to himself.

Everything was working perfectly. Like clockwork, Len shutoff his car engine, under the cover of the hospital's parking complex, at eight fifty-three. Len then struggled with the flowers to get them up to Tracie's floor in the hospital. His struggles put him a little behind schedule but getting to the floor three minutes late seemed insignificant to him.

Stepping off of the elevator, Len spotted Tracie's nurse from the night before. He made eye contact with her and was greeted with a smile in return.

"Wow!" The nurse commented on the flowers Len dragged into the ward.

"I've been told that if it's worth doing then it's worth doing it right," Len replied pointing to the flowers.

"Well they're in there waiting on you," the nurse said through a smile.

I walked over to the door and stood in the doorway of Tracie's room unnoticed by Tracie. The baby and Tracie were beautiful together. The baby was sprawled out atop Tracie nursing quietly at her chest.

After a few moments, Tracie must have felt my presence at the door. Tracie suddenly turned towards me dislodging herself from the baby's mouth.

"Len what are you doing over there and what is all of that you got?" Tracie inquired.

The baby quickly found Tracie's tit again and was settled back into her rhythmic suckling before I could say a word. I knew that Tracie loved surprises but can't stand to wait on them so without any fanfare, I tore open the paper around the large arrangement of flowers and laid them at Tracie's waist.

There were so many flowers that they extended from Tracie's waist, down to the foot of the bed, and overflowed onto the floor.

"Len you're wonderful! Come here and give me a kiss," Tracie implored me.

Woo ah! I thought to myself. Tracie's breath hit me a good six inches before my lips reached hers. It didn't matter. I kissed her full and deep wanting to share everything that she had.

"That was good! I haven't had one of those from you in over six months," Tracie amorously told me.

"I've been saving them up for you girl," I said with a smile, exhibiting my newfound confidence in her and the baby.

"You mean I've been missing all that? Mmm, I can't wait another six months. Give me another one of those boy."

I was all too happy to oblige. While I was giving her a second kiss, Tracie worked my dick through the thin wool fabric of my pants. Everybody in the room was satisfied.

No one had touched the one eyed monster for the six months since I had been with Tracie last. I couldn't control myself. In seconds the monster was out of control. An enormous wet stain instantly began soaking through the light tan fabric on my slacks.

The release was calming and placed me in a euphoric state. Before long my head was lying on Tracie's stomach, next to the baby, and my nose was smelling the aroma of fresh flowers.

"The nurse told me that you came by yesterday," Tracie said as she ran her fingers through my hair scattering if every which way.

"You were asleep and visiting hours were over, so I didn't bother you," I said in a low soft tone so as not to disrupt the baby or the groove that Tracie and I were in.

"Len, what are we going to do?"

"Well, I was thinking that you, baby Lyn, and I could live happily ever after," I said. My voice was still low but also chivalrous.

"Len, Baby Len has a name. Her name is Jamika Shanika."

No baby, Tracie, let's name her Lyn; you know "L" "Y" "N"," I replied in my same full of love tone."

"Ain't, no baby of mine gonna be named no Lyn. Her name is Jamika Shanika!" Tracie was loud, she jerked the baby in her tirade, and the baby started crying.

I could smell Tracie's breath from my now standing position, and it was repulsive.

Tracie forcibly moved the baby's head back to her chest in an effort to quiet her.

Regaining my composure, I sat down next to Tracie's bed. "Look you're asking me to accept a lot. If you want me to believe in you and baby Lyn, then name her Lyn Edwards; please."

Can you believe that I was almost begging her?

"Nope, her name is Jamika Shanika and that's final!"

Before I could get another word out of my mouth, a big black guy walked into the room smelling of cheap wine.

"Hey Tracie," the big black man said.

"How's little Jamika doing?"

I looked at the man good in the face, looked at Tracie, then at the baby. I must have looked at them all at least five times before I asked, "Who is this Tracie?"

"Oh, I'm sorry Len, this is Roc. Roc, this is Len."

I stared at Tracie waiting for further explanation. She felt my stare, and answered it.

"What! I told you that if I couldn't get what I needed from you, there's always someone waiting in the wings. Len, I didn't know what you were going to do!"

I just sat down in the chair, with my face in my hands, waiting for my shell to get strong. No baby of mine could ever be named Jamika Shanika. Right then and there, I knew that this could not be my baby. No! This isn't my baby.

The big black guy spoke out, "Hey man! I think you had an accident in your pants." He said this with a chuckle pointing to the crotch of my pants.

I didn't need to reply, my shell was back working on full. I quietly got up out of the chair and walked out of there. I haven't seen Tracie or her baby since.

EPILOGUE
SEVENTEEN YEARS LATER

Jamika and her friends were all getting ready to go out and party. She really didn't feel like going out on the town tonight.

But her friend O'ne, who just received the balance of her trust fund from her father's estate, wanted to go out and celebrate.

Jamika had just had it out with her mother Tracie again. All of her life she had asked her mother the same question. "Who is my daddy?"

For years her mother had avoided Jamika's questions about her father. This time when she asked her mother about her father, her mother slapped her.

"That son of a bitch wasn't nothing to write home about. He left our asses right there in Cook County Hospital. I ain't telling you shit about that mother fucker."

"Mama maybe he can help us," Jamika explained. Jamika was desperate. She felt like her life was falling apart. Over the last few years she had seen the fast life get the best of her mother. She needed the prince of a father that she had dreamed about over the years to come and save them.

Jamika was alone and she knew it. She needed her father.